MONSTERS AND MYSTERIES AROUND THE CORNER

CONNOR FLYNN

BEYOND THE FRAY

Publishing

BEYOND THE FRAY

Publishing

CONTENTS

CHAPTER 1
INITIATION

Monster hunter since a kid. At Universal Studios in
Orlando and that's Jaws behind me.

T he light burns our eyes but we are afraid of the
dark. I grew up reading books like Goose-
bumps and watching Tales from the Crypt, so
you can say I was built for this. I think that we all were,
we all question our reality but only some are brave

enough to do something about it. Believe in it or not, the other side will reveal herself in the moments when we least expect. So climb the wall now, so we can plan for what's on the other side of this fence. Heaven is real, but so are monsters. Mysteries are right around the corner, lock your doors.

Do you remember being born? I have memories in the womb and still can visualize my baptism. I have written down my dreams for decades and have gathered as much info on the other side as I can. I rode around on the fire truck responding to calls as a kid. I used to spend nights in the barn sleeping on the hay bails talking to the animals. While hiking, biking, and fishing, I'm searching for fossils and monsters! I rather find them before they find me!

My family has always been full of explorers and freedom fighters. On my mother's side I am connected to Thomas Jefferson and on my dad's side, I'm related to our greatest president. I have visited the site in Dallas where my Fitzgerald family lost one member. The evil people in power have censored the truth and eliminated our patriots. It is my duty to my family bible and Irish blood to continue my descendants path of destiny.

I heard a story from David Paulides that took place in 1868. The name caught my attention. Katie Flynn went missing while riding a horse in Michigan. She was two. Her path merged with tracks of a black bear. Two hunters joined the search with her parents and they couldn't find her all night. The next day they heard a cry through some brush. They saw a monster creature jump into the river and disappeared into the dark. Katie was found with bad scratches on her face and hands. Most likely from being hit by branches at high speeds.

In the Garden of Eden, the edge of the old continent.

Katie said the big dog took her in his arms and walked away with her. The "big dog" ate her one missing shoe. The big black thing came and played with her initially. It even brought her wintergreen berries. The creature carried Katie, laid her on a bed of leaves and kept her warm. She was unharmed. A bear would not do this. Many blamed it on a pack of wolves but you know what I believe... I plan to gain ground on the mystery of my last name.

My dad is a paramedic and fireman. My mom is either fishing or researching our ancestry. My sister has saved lives as a lifeguard and also survived a coma. My mom's fiancé is a trucker and my step mom is a nurse. My step sister once stopped a man from jumping off a bridge. My dad's parents were immigrants from Ireland. My Pepa was a Marine and my mom's mother has Cree blood. My aunt once witnessed a banshee in Ireland as a young girl. You can say it's in my blood to explore for more. You can catch me in the salt caves or a sensory deprivation chamber seeking enlightenment

Ancient structures still cannot be figured out or recreated, even with the world's most advanced technology. Geoglyphs that are hundreds of feet in length depict humanoid creatures have shown up all the known continents of the new world. They were created long before the usage of planes so the real question is who were they built for? We look to hieroglyphs and ancient tablets for clues of our past but only get more questions. Meditation and psychedelics open up new doors but some hallways need to be walked through.

We don't have to travel all the way to Egypt or Greece to reach holy land, it's right under our feet! The states have pyramids and temples of their own. There are tens of thousands of ancient structures and burial mounds filled with clues to our ancestors' past. Thousands of giant skeletons were excavated when America paved the roads and sadly a museum I once respected, has gone to great lengths to erase our history. I'm still waiting on an explanation of crop circles! In many villages across the world, they believe people live inside giant boulders and they build the roads around them. This is expensive and would only be done for a reason.

One of my family friends growing up was tragically killed. They ruled it a suicide but there was many inconsistencies in the case. Many speculated that he had cooperated with police and they did not want to admit that they failed to protect him. A kid that used to ride my bus has claimed to have gotten away with his murder and it tears me up inside that government cover ups like The Adjustment Bureau are closer to home than one might think.

Remnants of our past are either ash or at the bottom of the ocean. But luckily, the truth will always surface. Hikers and explorers stumble upon our hidden history every day. The plasma of our existence and consciousness are still forever expanding. Paranormal is just normal. The forest comes alive at night and there are certainly unidentified flying objects in the sky. Pack a personal GPS locator beacon and be safe while adventuring! I hope you packed extra water for this one! And if we run into a vortex of electromagnetic energy, please remain calm and just try to follow me. I've done this before…

I grew up urban exploring and trailblazing by natural trade. I was always fishing new spots with my mom, preparing for hunts with Pepa and visiting new cities with my dad. I was the Pinewood Derby champ in the boy scouts and Memorial Olympic medalist in Mohican. I love venturing to wild spots off the grid with friends after dark and eating at haunted diner and bars. I've met Zydrunas Ilgauskaus and seen Yao Ming with my own two eyes. The giant gene is still alive in our community.

Growing up in Ohio, I was surrounded by stories of the Grassman, the mistakes on the lake, and thousands of ancient burial mounds. I grew up fishing for the Lake Erie Monster, journeying through Helltown, and hunting the Frogmen. We picked many berries, hunted ginseng, and searched for mushrooms. The state is flooded with haunted colleges and cry baby bridges. Mansfield Reformatory and Moundsville Prison shaped my expectations of gothic marvels.

After twenty-three years, I moved down to Florida after refereeing the National Flag Football Championships in Polk County. I lived out of my car and with that came many adventures. I joined a punk rock musical and became the stage manager. We played many shows in the Tampa area and even had a close run in with the

Seminole Heights serial killer. That summer we survived the road to the west coast and encountered many anomalies. Luckily, I had a sturdy tent and couchsurfed with many incredible people.

After Hurricane Irma, I moved to the Panhandle to be closer to my mom's ranch. I got a job at the famous local bowling alley amusement park and a gig umpiring local baseball and softball games. We had a boat that we took out when we weren't fishing on her pond. We picked pecans and other fruit, selling bags to locals. It was a nice change of pace.

The Grassy Knoll, Dallas, Texas...where everything changed.

Tragically, the strongest hurricane to ever make landfall in the country struck our town directly. It did severe damage to my trailer but luckily I made it to my mom's. Sadly she watched most of her fruit trees fall and the land was forever changed. The storm killed countless people but luckily our family and friends were safe physically. We were scared mentally but have bound together for the bounce back. The lanes were destroyed but I was determined to find something else that fit me.

My search for the paranormal is an inward journey. It's incredibly fulfilling when you crack the code and find a couple cookie crumbs. I have learned so much about the possibilities this terra has to offer and even more about myself. This is a deeper dive into my collection of data and notes that I have been journaling since at least 2000. Been keeping tabs on my dreams and strange experiences ever since I could hold a pen with my right to write. I was there when Cookie Carrasco returned from battling leukemia, I know what magic looks like.

I am on a quest for consciousness and trying to see what my twenty-one grams has to offer. Energy is never created, nor destroyed. It has always existed. Coincidence is the only thing to never exist and a penny saved is only one cent. Every song, story, and script that I work on represents the land beyond the poles that are probably looking for us too. I will continue to look for the deer people on my drive to work but you just focus on not texting while driving! Sometimes I believe seatbelts are a conspiracy but that debate is for another day... There's a knock at my door! Shoot!

CHAPTER 2
BOSTON ROAD
MEDINA / CUYAHOGA COUNTY LINE, OHIO

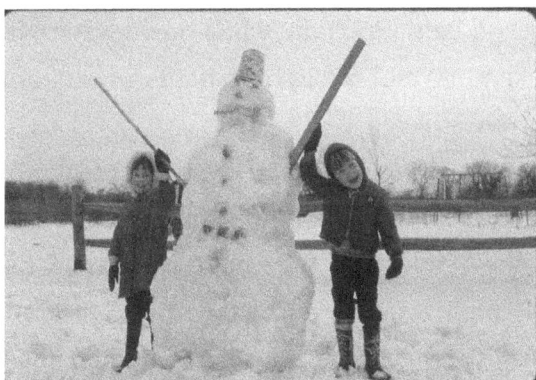

My mom and her twin.

G rowing up, my friends always believed my house was haunted but I knew it first hand. There were creaks in the floorboards, rattling in the laundry room, and footsteps in the attic. The surrounding area is all forest and there used to be an airport deep in the woods. There are two small mounds in the backyard and I have proof that they have special energy. Some of my friends blamed my collection of game used sports memorabilia. They said the collectibles and deer head were cursed! My mom grew up in the house and had many strange experiences as well.

When she was growing up, there were far less houses and a lot more forests. There used to be drag races on the dirt paths back behind my house. Gangs of people would hang out burning fires in garbage cans after dark. They would chase their unwanted visitors with knives and baseball bats. One time while on vacation, the house was broken into and my grandparents jewelry and video camera were stolen.

PePa was a Marine and these people had broken more than one unwritten rule in his book. They trespassed, they stole, and they have threatened his livelihood. No night would ever be the same. My grandfather got a dog to watch the house. He trained the pup to protect the family and they became best friends.

Under the hounds watch, there were no more burglaries but my mom remembers a couple strange occurrences. The dog would often growl towards the woods at all hours of the night. He refused to bark at this presence. When suspicious people or other dogs passed by, he let them hear it. My mom remembered thinking it may have been a wolf or pack of coyotes.

My mom's twin brother's bedroom was the room that I grew up in. One window faced a large patch of woods and the other was perched by the apple and pear trees. Over a span of forty years, we both experienced strange occurrences within those four walls.

X-Games mode.

My uncle had been woken up by the sound of finger-nails scraping on the glass. My grandparents would blame it on tree limbs and the wind but my uncle knew there was something more to it. He had also spotted large shadow creatures peeking in through the night. He thought monsters lived across the creek and said sometimes the lights would flicker. I had very similar encounters.

One night, my parents went out with some friends to the Eagles Club. They ordered us some pizza and told us to not open the door for anyone. I was downstairs playing Xbox with Matt when we thought pounding on the back door. Then suddenly, my sister and Kalie come downstairs crying. They said someone was trying to break into the house.

We crept upstairs and now there was loud knocking up front. I peaked out the window and couldn't see a thing. Then more pounding out back. We ran to the back-door and turned on the porch light. Still nothing.

We opened the door and yelled out to stop messing with us. My sister and Kalie locked themselves in the bathroom and were begging for us to join. Matt and I continued investigating. But when each door knob was shaking simultaneously and we heard loud smacks on the garage, we decided to hide in the shower as well. We stayed locked up for a couple hours and luckily survived until the parents got back.

One day after school, I saw my cat laying dead in the road. I pulled up, grabbed her body and laid her in the grass. I wept and cried while digging a hole to bury her in. She was laid to rest by the mound in my backyard. I punched a hole in my shower after I called both my parents to tell her the news. I went to court for a speeding ticket and lost my license. When I got home, my mom called my name and Baby was laying in her bed. I was so relieved.

Years later, in the summer after midnight I was on my way home from work at Family Video and saw something crossing the road up ahead of me. It was the intersection of Prospect and Boston Road. A popular crossing spot for deer between two huge patches of woods near a stream that was a tributary of Rocky River. This was no deer, this was a bipedal creature.

I recently found out that there is a "witches stone" in the woods located right by that crossing. A writer that my mom used to babysit told me he had many mythical encounters in those same woods. He had run-ins with ghosts, goblins, and poachers back on the trails. He wrote many tales based on his childhood in Beebetown.

I shined my brights and saw a strange creature that reminded me of gollum from Lord of the Rings or the crawlers from The Descent. It had the same color skin as a deer but moved like a hunchback man. I saw long wrinkles and its veins through the skin. It continued into the woods to the right toward my house and really had me spooked. I had to beat it home.

The Whitney Road monster picture was taken just across town and looks similar to what I encountered... The creature had long sprawling fingers like a grey alien cave monster. The monster had to be four to six feet tall and very skinny. I could see his ribs and bones. He looked hungry but still very powerful and mean. It may have been a Skinwalker. That or a naked hungry man.

There was a very strange mist and feeling as I drove by. Almost put me into a trance. I have thought about it every time that I drove passed ever since.. It was no surprise that that patch of woods always had an eerie vibe. The creek flowed into 252 and Rocky River. We always saw deer and heard coyote activity. When we would sneak out at night, we'd always keep an eye on the wood line.

Whenever I hosted parties or campfires, we always heard weird screams and bellows coming from the woods across the street from my house in the middle of the night and it would terrorize my friends. But early in the morning when I would be at the bottom of the driveway waiting all alone for the bus in the freezing dark windy mornings, I'd hear whispers in the wind coming from the forest and tunnel under the road. That was the worst. It was always very misty in the morning. The fog was so thick that sometimes I couldn't see my porch.

We also always had stories about the haunted red house across the street. The old cabin sat back in the woods and was either empty or changing residents every other month. In the dark early mornings, I always kept an eye on the front door and the windows. Some nights you'd see shadows or glowing lights in the gaps.

As a grade schooler, I envisioned a beast or murderous man storming out and running after me. I always timed it in my head so I could either make it to my front door or the neighbors by the time he made it to the street. That man still finds his way into my nightmares from time to time.

I was friends with some of the temporary tenants Jamie and Grace. They were brother and sister to some poor parents. Grace would come over and ask to use our restroom. She would either say hers was broken or she didn't want to go into the basement. She said the witch in the woods sneaks in through the basement windows. They didn't last long at the red house.

Another time, my friends and I were riding bikes in the streets behind my house. We played in the creek and explored the woods. One time, this white van was following us. The driver turned around multiple times when we switched directions and pursued us relentlessly.

We ended up splitting up and taking off into the woods. We met up in a known spot and waited it out until dark. We still wonder what that white van wanted and I still have strange flashbacks about those woods, the house across the street and hidden streets behind my house where the airport once stood.

In the early development of the roads, my friend Charlie and I were riding our bikes to explore some of the reserve ponds. We heard some gunshots in the distance but thought nothing of it and kept fishing. We noticed these two black figures approaching us from a long open field. After a while we could see that they were giant dogs and they were gaining on us. We pedaled as fast as we could but saw that they would catch us eventually and we could not afford that.

We ditched our bikes and ran into the woods. We had to find the creek, we could follow it home. There was a giant fallen tree and we climbed the large roots for security. We armed ourselves with limbs and braced for these demon dogs to attack. They hunted us down. The mightyena houndoom hybrids were closing in.

The wolves were foaming at the mouth and letting off monstrous growls. We were shaking in fear. They circled us sniffing and staring us down. Covered in black fur and had really long legs.They stalked us for what felt like hours before taking off into the woods. We think someone shot at them and that the creatures were just running confused. Thankfully they sensed that we didn't want any problems.

Years later, I was having a girl sleepover and my mom was still home. So I asked her to park in the development on the edge of the woods so my mom wouldn't see her car in the drive. I promised to wait outside for her and walk her back to my house. The girl was running late and I was getting restlessly aimlessly waiting for her.

Her phone was going straight to voicemail so I left a couple of them. I sat back down in anger. I waited some more. Then an eerie feeling swept over me. I stood up. I heard something shuffling in the woods. I took one step closer and then it bolted right towards me. I turned as hard as I could to run as fast as my body would let me. It was near pitch black and I couldn't see a thing but I knew what direction home was. I got up to full speed but it was still hunting after me. Then boom, I felt a sharp pain in my shoulder and my face but still kept running.

I almost added myself to my neighbors compost pile. I ran full speed into a tall stake and the rod had stabbed me right through my lip and face. It had also fractured my collarbone. I felt like Ray Lewis had hit me going over the middle. I crawl for a second then focus on getting back to my feet.. I stumbled to my yard and high tailed it to the back door. Locked it behind me and sprawled downstairs. I was in a daze for a good while until my phone rang and snapped me out of it. It was the girl.

She had just pulled up and was out there looking for me. I told her to get back in the car and drive as fast as she could. She laughed and asked me what I was talking about. I told her something was out there and I just got attacked. She told me to give it up and just kept nagging.

This stubborn hag wasn't listening. I ran out there and once she saw my face, she went right towards the car. I didn't hear from her for a while but I was more worried about how long I had to wear this damn sling for and to make sure my face didn't get infected!

Summers later, I was camping in my backyard with J bird. We were in the back stargazing when something caught our eye. It was a red amber glow that was vibrating enough for us to notice. It felt like it sucked our attention right in. After what felt like a lifetime, we both said, "Are you seeing this?"

First day of school in Brunswick, Ohio.

Once we both collectively engaged, it started to play tricks on our mind. It went from a dot to a line and was having us track it. It was telepathic and made me feel connected to something much bigger. We encountered the red eye other times over the years but that very first time there was a true connection.

Down the road, Stefan Prince lived at the bottom of Boston hill. He called in the 2008 BHS bomb threat and left voicemails threatening something worse than Columbine. I still remember riding the high school bus as an eighth grader going to early bird Spanish class finding out what was going on. I was confused when I saw the swat team and was totally lost. A pro motocross racer came from his foster home too, I always looked for them when I passed the property.

Just up the hill, there is a legend of a ghost at the intersection of Pearl and Boston Road. There was a deadly crash there more than fifty years ago and my family remembers it. There are reports of flashing lights and specters appearing. My best friend Bird and his mother had an encounter decades ago. They saw a dark shadow figure dash across Pearl from the high ridges and vanish into the high shrub as they went up the hill towards Boston. His mom told the story when we were young and I searched ever since.

I've had a lot of action near the Beebetown Cemetery on Marks Road near the intersection of Boston. There is a known haunted house nearby and I always stared into the windows as my school bus passed. Another time a crazy lady followed us home beeping because we went first at a stop sign a few roads back. We tricked her and juked her in a cul-de-sac. Probably a reincarnation of Martha Wise or the Stoskopf Witch.

Between the cemetery and my house, Bird and I were driving late at night approaching the blinking red lights at the intersection. At that time, there was a huge buzz around the town of the Brunswick Beast. It was rumored to be a monster blue chupacabra. Many kids in the high school claimed to have spotted the beast near the town lake. Well, I tell you that BB is not blue. But when we both spotted it, it truly looked like the goat sucker. The strange creature washed up in front of our car like a baby deer. I wonder if this was the only we crossed paths.

Sadly in 2012, my city lost four of the brightest young kids on the night before graduation. Four kids, and three of my close friends sadly passed away in a car accident on the Boston Road railroad pass. The railroad gate created a huge bump that acted as a ramp for cars. It was very dangerous. My friends were heading to Witches Ball and Erma's house but decided to hit the pass. That night forever reshaped the families lives and the way of our city. They reshaped the railroad crossing but sadly the damage had been done.

When I moved out to go to college, my sister had some bad people on the property. They made themselves at home and showed no respect. It was really tough when I would come back for the weekend for holiday. After my sister moved out, our house got broken into multiple times and we believe it was some of them. That really messed with my sanity and I worried about my mom. It had a lot to do with us moving out of Ohio.

CHAPTER 3
THE MYSTERIES OF THE METROPARKS
CUYAHOGA COUNTY, OHIO

Jake in the jungle.

T he Cleveland MetroParks Zoo is the largest in the state. The metro parks are an extensive system of nature preserves in the greater Cleveland area. The region holds many rivers, dense forests, and vast wildlife. There are many golf courses and even a castle to explore. Boo at the Zoo sweeps the city during October but there are a couple real life hauntings that are active for all four seasons down in the valley! Take heed!

I spent my childhood all throughout the Metro Parks. I'd watch my dad's football games, golf the par 3 courses and I even had my graduation party in the valley. I have road many miles on the trails, caught some smallmouth bass out of Rocky River, and refereed many games at Brookside. In the winter we enjoyed walking on the river and the toboggan chutes at Chalet. We always saw many deer and rarely heard stories about bears in the forest. I imagined a wild Ursaring (a bear type Pokemon) tearing through camp.

My good friend Ripple is about twenty years my elder. We met in Florida and realized we were both from Cleveland. He used to sneak into Squire's Castle at night and spend the night there with his friends. They would invite girls and get drunk in the gothic mansion. He shook when he said some unexplainable things occurred. He claimed doors slammed, flashlights died, and they were chased by police and mysterious forces on multiple occasions.

I had heard of so many legends down in the valley so I always kept my eyes on the forest when riding shotgun in my dad's white grand prix. I knew there were Sasquatch sightings along 252, deep caves at Whipps Ledges and ghosts along Brookside. But I couldn't have imagined that the nightmares from those legends crept through the woods near my front window at night when I slept!

Under the waterfall at Bear Cave

One midnight, we snuck onto a golf course to fish some ponds for exotic fish. They stock the ponds with monster sized rare breeds. We parked in a cul-de-sac and trekked through the woods on a course straight to one of the later holes. The moon was bright but the canopy of trees made the area feel bleak like a horror movie. We moved on with our gear and made it to the ponds.

We fished for a couple hours and caught countless fish. The entire time we kept an ear out for motors and an eye out for lights. We were trying to be quiet but the occasional giggle and snort amplified through the night. We enjoyed the chorus of crickets as we blew smoke into the air. We were beginning to pack up when we heard something that made us turn our lights off and rush outta there.

We heard voices from a couple hundred yards away. We figured someone must have called the police on us. There was no way the groundskeeper was out this late. Maybe someone saw us park and enter the woods. They could have easily connected the dots. They might have thought we were sabotaging the greens.

We took off into the woods and still heard the sounds approaching. We kept up our pace but could barely see. I called my friend Brian and whispered to him that some-body was following us. He lived nearby and I wanted him to drive to our car. But that didn't make sense. Mostly I wanted him to know where we were. I felt bad about waking him up but was truly panicking.

We didn't use our lights because that would be a dead giveaway. We climbed up this steep hill and the dirt was sliding down making it very difficult. We looked back and saw glimmers of light pointing in our direction.

We had been spotted and we had no choice but to run. That's when my next level kicked in.

Stones and mud filled up my shoes and I lost some gear but I was gaining ground on the incline. I was scared they were going to shoot us in the back. Were these police or poachers? Adam fell behind and I was worried they were going to capture him. I got to the top of the ridge and began hurling rocks above Adam and 4. I helped them up and we bolted toward the edge of the trees.

Our car was still there and we all hopped in. We drove home safely and didn't see one police car. We debated if there was anything out there at all. What voices were we hearing? What were those glowing lights under the canopy? Something ushered us out of there with just a little effort of recommendation.

Years later, I was hiking with 4 and his buddy Ty at Cascade Park in Elyria. We were excited to climb Pink Floyd Rock and see the two giant waterfalls. I was hoping the boys would be down to scale the ruins to see the best spot in the park and feel the vibration of the raging waters below. We had a spliff to spark in the bear cave and I had my go pro camera to capture the adventure.

We coasted down the steep entrance to the park. It reminded me of the spiral canyon in Diddy Kong Racing. I've had a couple nightmares like that over the years. I don't know if being the passenger or the driver is worse. I think I prefer having control and we all know what it feels like to drive or run in a dream. We pulled up to the parking lot and gave a head nod to the group next to us. Elyria always had some interesting characters. I always believed cool places brought cool people but sometimes I should think twice.

Ty Cobb carving.

One of the guys in the group followed us for a bit and asked us for a lighter. We tossed him it and told him to keep it. We took off down the trail exploring ledges and all the graffiti. We kept an eye out for deer and searched the cracks for snakes. We jumped in surprise when a black cat leaped from a tree and took off up the steep hillside. We laughed and took off down the river to the waterfall. We eyed up the cave below and b lined it there.

Ty told us that they used to keep bears in this cave. I closed my eyes and the vibrations of the water took me to the past. The roaring beasts were right next to me but I was one of them. They brushed up beside me as we enjoyed the same cascade pouring from above. I snapped out of it when they nudged it, passing me the blunt. We ducked and climbed the rocks below. I filmed some with my go pro but weirdly the battery died quickly. We kept an eye out for police or for people that could report us.

We saw somebody approaching so we finished up and started investigating the cave walls. They were marked up from the past years. We crawled out and took off toward the trail to the next waterfall and ruins. We noticed the person was the guy from before. Ty and 4 both were both uneasy and thought he was an under-cover. They were mad that I gave him the lighter.

We sped up and kept walking. He suddenly comes up from the other direction and approaches me directly. He has a big smile on his face and is acting like he knows me. He goes to shake my hand and give me a bro hug. He politely asks me how I have been and I try to play it cool but I really don't recognize him. His tone changes a bit and he questions if I'm going to ask him if I'm going to introduce him to my friends. I hesitate and he says, "C'mon Connor".

That's when everything changed. How did this guy know my name? He didn't go to my school and I didn't recognize him on the music scene. Did he hear them call me by name? He couldn't have. We all paused for a second, he forced a handshake on Ty and got his name. He asked 4 and 4 put up 4 fingers. He asked us if we wanted to smoke at the ruins but I told him that we had to roll out. He interrogated us why we took this trail then and 4 spoke up. We turned to go and he called out "What about you Ty? They can pick you up!"

We hustled back to the parking lot and the same group was there. We barely looked at them but clear as day, we saw the guy that was harassing us. His eyes were black and his gang all resembled him. We skirted out of there and argued in the car afterward. I thought he was a Skinwalker or vampire. But Ty thought he was a cop or spy. Then he accused me of being an informant or something. 4 thought I owed the guy money and that's why I bailed. I think they were both under a spell. He was trying to get Ty alone. What was with that? He was trying to conquer us and already had us divided.

CHAPTER 4
SLEEPOVER AT SAM'S
MEDINA, OHIO

Overhang near Sam's.

here are thousands of active serial killers in this country but I'm most at risk at one of my best friend's homes. The Passafiume residence was the haunted house on the hill with the winding driveway that all the scary horror movies are based on. Faces in the windows greeting newcomers is just the tip of the blade. With a mysterious past, deep wells, and a dark cellar, the walls had all the elements they needed. Screams in your dreams, pictures watching you in the hallway, and whispers from the attic keep all visitors walking on eggshells from morning to night time.

I met Sam playing Fall Ball in Medina. He was one of the best baseball players I had ever shared the field with. We were on the Thunder and the team was made up with kids from Brunswick and Medina. Sam's a couple years younger and was playing "Up", he had earrings and a necklace so I thought he was a troublemaker at first. When he first shook hands with me, he called me sir. We played catch and the friendship was bonded.

We had a game later in the week and after a good practice, the new team was fired up to hit the diamond. I dapped up Sam before he walked over to his mom's old classic ride. I rode home with Scotty and talked about how we thought the season would go. We had high hopes after we both had a good regular season with the Marlins and we upgraded our roster. Scott approved of the new players as well.

The first game came and it was going as planned until the last inning. The coach's son in right field had a couple errors and allowed the other team to tie the game up. There were two outs and still guys on second and third base when there was a blast over my head in center.

I misjudged it and just stuck my glove out Willy Mays style and felt the ball land in the webbing while tumbling over into the fence. I stood up and held the ball up! The team went crazy! I walked my next at bat, stole second, and got driven in by Sam's hit that just barely missed clearing the fence! We did it. We won!

Sam invited me to sleepover that night and of course I obliged. His mom was cooking out and I was always down for an adventure. On the way over there, she warned me of the mess. I told her that I had no problem with it. Sam warned me that it was haunted. Now that I may raise some worries.

We pulled into the long steep curved driveway and Sam pointed toward the window and asked what I saw. I thought it was a trick because I saw a young boy clear as day. I asked if that was his little brother and Sam started screaming that I could see him too. Sam said the boy used to live at the home many years ago and they hear him playing in the house at all hours of the night.

Sam's mom explained that the activity was very reactive. The ghosts only were present when you gave them attention. She advised not to think about them but how could I not when I just saw a little boy in the window. I was in full Paranormal Activity mode and that was going to stir up the energy for the night.

Sam gave me a tour of his home and yard. He showed me his baseball memorabilia, his man cave basement, and huge backyard. We grabbed a pop from the kitchen and he said one time all the drawers and cabinets flew open and made a ruckus. There was a picture of his mom on the wall and it was when she was younger. She was modeling and looking beautiful but it caught my eye for another reason. It felt like she was staring at me. Trying to tell me something.

Time passed and after dinner we went outside to make a fire. We had all the supplies for s'mores and Sam had a surprise for me. It was three axe cans taped together. I was roasting my marshmallow when he tossed it in and it started hissing. I ran away just in time when there was a huge mushroom cloud explosion. It was big enough to wake the living and the DEAD!

We stayed out there for hours telling scary stories and sneaking shots of the old basement whisky. Sam went in to get more drinks while I had to go to the bathroom. I went over to the pool and started peeing beside it. I heard a subtle splashing and looked back over my shoulder. I thought I saw something dive underwater when I heard a crash in the forest.

I took off running while still going to the bathroom. I made a mess on the front of my pants and came stumbling back toward the fire. Sam was just waking up and was dying of laughter. He asked "The pool or the woods?" I yelled "Both!" while I collapsed in the chair.

He shook his head and snarled that he told me to stay by the fire!

We crawled inside and got the basement ready for bedtime. He turned on a movie and Sam was asleep in minutes. I was laying wide awake with the room spinning. I was trying my best to just breathe out the alcohol and try to tell myself that I would be okay. That's when I heard some noises coming from the laundry room. I figured it was the washer or dryer running but then I heard one door open.

I tried to ignore it but there was a faint whispering in my ear. The energy was calling my name and pulling me toward the dark room. I got off the air mattress and started slithering on the ground in that direction. Each inch I crept near, the better I felt. But I knew that wasn't necessarily a good thing. I got to the opening of the door and I was finally able to stand up.

I wiggled over to the washer ever so slowly. It sounded like the whispers were coming from inside. The door was flipped open up and I was just steps from being able to look in. A huge whiff of sulfur hit my nose when I noticed the washer was filling up. I peeked my eyes over the edge and noticed it was blood. I went to close the door and a hand rose up and grabbed my arm. The top slammed down as I ran back toward bed. Sam just murmured "Go to bed!"

I must have passed out from the fear because I don't

remember the rest of the night. I recall Sam waking me up in the morning with breakfast and a special smoothie calling it the "Hangover Cure". His mom asked if we slept all right and I hesitated. She knew something happened. She said that some of the spirits were soothing and guardian angels. And I laughed "Not this one.

"Years later, I went over Sam's for a cookout and spent the night after. It was basically the same routine. Adventuring around the property and a nighttime fire with some drinks. Sam said the encounters continued over the years but would go ghost for months. They had psychics and mediums visit to contact the spirits. They heard replies from a family named "The Steins".

Sam mentioned a recent encounter that scared him pretty badly. He heard a loud crash in the night that woke him up. He went over to the den and saw his grandfather's love seat was flipped over. Sam took this as a personal attack and was pretty messed up for a couple of weeks. He shared all of this around the fire as the eyes in the forest watched us.

After everyone went home, Sam and I were cleaning up outside when we heard a whistle from the woods. The hair on the back of my neck rose up but I continued like I didn't notice anything. I peeked over to Sam and he was doing the same. Then came another whistle from the opposite side of the wood line. There were multiple creatures out there and they were communicating. Sam and I looked at each other, dumped the garbage in the fire and ran toward his cellar.

We locked the door behind us and cracked open a few more drinks. I pointed to the laundry room and told Sam about my nocturnal encounter. He was stunned and said he has had nightmares of that same washer overflowing with blood. The rest of the night was pretty relaxing. Luckily, we fell asleep quickly and I wasn't haunted by any bad dreams and night terrors.

The next morning I had Sam's special smoothie and was feeling great. We smoked a joint at the picnic table and stared off into the trees. He joked that they are a lot less scary during the day. At night, branches become arms and normal trees become weir woods with talking faces. I gave my brother a hug and got in my car. As I pulled out of his driveway, I looked in my rear view mirror and saw the little boy I'm the window waving goodbye when I first saw him. See you later buddy, remember to close the drawers and wear your life jacket!

CHAPTER 5
THE TOWN UNDER TAPPAN LAKE
LACEYVILLE, OHIO

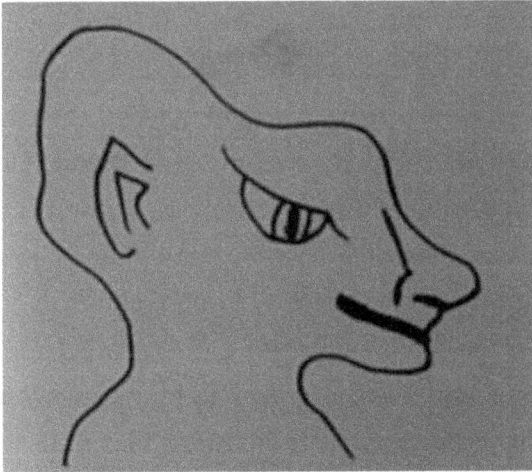

The Goblin of the Lake

f you have seen the movie Lost River, then you know the vibe of Tappan Lake. Underneath the murky depths is the town of Laceyville, full of forgotten memories and flooded dreams. The surrounding area is full of deep valleys and tree stands, where crime gets handled internally. Bodies have been dumped, cabins have been burned, and people have vanished and I am starting to wonder if the town is cursed like Lost River.

My family had a trailer near Tappan Lake. We loved visiting during the summer and spending a couple nights out in the woods. We would hike, fish, and of course take the boat out on the water. My grandfather would bring us over his hunting buddy's house and introduce us to all their domesticated animals. I made many friends at the beach but my best friend found us.

There was a knock on the door and it was the neighbors. They were frantic and couldn't find their son. His name was Max and he was my best friend. He loved adventuring and animals just as much as my sister and I. I hadn't seen him since the day before but I had an idea where he might have been.

While the adults searched and screamed for Max, I started to follow the creek. We had built some small forts along the water and he loved spending time with the beavers at the dam. We had seen bobcats and other predators in the area so I wanted to link up with him as fast I could. There were legends of moonshiners and monsters in those hills so I was a bit nervous for Max but I knew he could fend for himself against most of the elements.

I got to the dam but he was nowhere in sight. I called out for his name and made some of our nature calls. I sat on a log waiting staring down the valley cliffs. The surrounding forest was silent. It was chilling. A storm was brewing and the energy was being bottled up on the hillside. I had to find his trial before the rains washed away his tracks.

It started violently raining so I crawled into a tree that we've been carving out over the years. The thunder was roaring and lightning strikes were tearing up the trees nearby. After watching LOST, the giant smoke monster reminded me a lot of those scary moments. But as swift as it crept it, the storm swept out. I still remained in the tree shaking and trembling in fear. Then I heard one of our nature calls.

It was Max, it had to be. I ran toward the noise and started calling his name. I expected to see him running towards me but heard nothing, saw nothing. I circled around confused and became very dizzy. I almost passed out when out of the corner of my eye, I saw Max crouched under a falling tree root. I stumbled over to him and he grabbed me and pulled me under. He put his hand over my mouth and said, "It's out there".

I'm not sure how much time passed but it was getting dark and Max knew we wouldn't survive the night out there. He woke me up from my trance and told me we had to go. He told me to follow him close and never look back. We ran through the woods at full speed many times before but never in the dark. He reiterated "Find the creek, you'll hear my feet!"

He took off running and I tried my best to keep up. The moment we left the tree, I heard a couple noises following behind in the brush. My mind exploded with possibilities. I questioned why he would tell me not to look back. What's so dangerous about seeing a bear or a big cat? But then I heard a noise I couldn't explain. That was no animal.

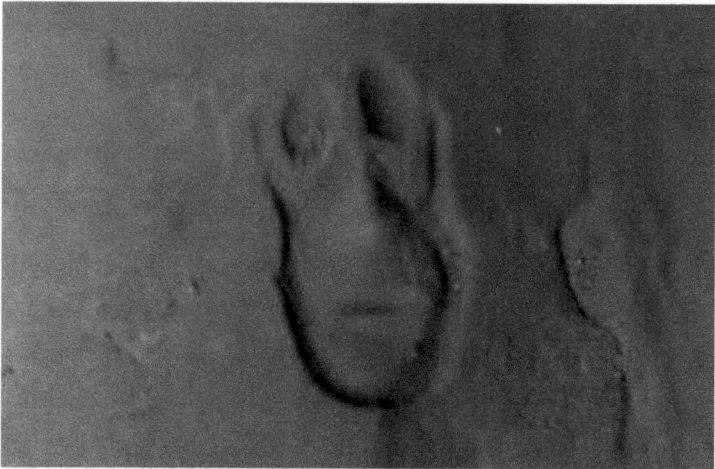

Goblin carving

Max heard the whispers and picked up the pace. We jumped over fallen trees on the path and launched off the path into the creek. We ran through the water at a full sprint but could still hear the voices approaching from behind. Luckily we knew the path home but it sounded like there were a full herd of them hunting us down.

We could hear them splashing in the creek, swinging in the trees and even more of them approaching on land. When I laid eyes on the edge of the tree line, my mind finally needed some answers. I knew Max told me not to look but sadly I defied him. I did a quick 180 turn of my head and met eyes with one of the forest demons.

Instantly I regretted my mistake. I was still thirty yards from the wood line and that was about twenty-five too many. I felt like he looked straight into my soul. He had black eyes and was very small. He was running the tree branches and moving very swiftly. He looked determined. He looked like we had upset him.

My knees gave out and I fell to the ground. My life flashed before my eyes and I soon expected to be swarmed by at least ten of them. The night elf launched from about twenty feet up and was heading straight for me. His fangs were exposed and nasty slime drool was coming from the sides of his mouth. I braced for impact when Max slammed in between and there was a huge collision. I rolled over and they all let out a sickening screech that pierced my ears.

Multiple climbed onto Max and started clawing and biting him. I ran over to help and was tackled to the ground. They were going to rip us to shreds. I fought back only hoping that Max would somehow save me. I knew I was done for but rather die here than be taken alive. I screamed and wrestled with the creatures when suddenly they let me go.

I saw Max standing up with something in his hand. They were circling around him with a gaze in their eyes. Max had some kind of sacred stone in his palm and it had the clan hypnotized. The forest dwarves seemed to be after the stone and not us. The leader moved towards Max and peacefully took the totem out from his fingers.

They nodded to us before backing off into the darkness. Max picked me up and apologized for putting me into danger. But then thanked me saying that he was lucky I showed up. He didn't think they would have let him live for stealing one of their ceremonial tokens.

He cried out that he didn't think they would have minded just one gem when they had a cave full. We both realized that the stones held much more importance than just simple wealth. They had spiritual value and held power over this species of hobbit people. We both agreed that we would never steal from or intentionally disrupt the forest children again.

As we walked back to the trailers, a swarm of memories flooded my mind. We had crossed paths with the forest gnomes in the past. It now explained the unexpected knocking on my windows, our minnow trap being scavenged, and the dogs barking at all hours of the night. They had been watching us all these years and we never had any problems until we crossed the line.

The parents rushed to us as we approached. They hugged Max and thanked me for finding him. We didn't even know where to begin so we said I found him near the beaver dam waiting out the rain. The story didn't explain the scratch claw and teeth marks but the parents were just happy he was back home safely. They called me a hero but it was actually Max who saved me, well after I saved him first...

Years later, our trailer was broken into and totally stripped clean. Everything was stolen and the walls had holes where they stole all the copper. We are not sure if it was the goblins or just some hillbilly tweakers. My grandparents were heartbroken and after our home was ravaged, our trips to Tappan Lake were never the same. My time around Laceyville changed when Max broke the golden rule.

I truly doubt the fae were the ones who destroyed our sanctuary because they seemed to have no problem with us after we returned the relic. After my time at Tappan Lake, I forever look at gnomes, leprechauns, and pixies with caution. I learned to never insult or interrupt the species if I encountered them and that time works differently when crossing their paths. It is common to lose hours or even days in their presence. Max was gone for almost a full day and it only felt like a couple hours to him.

I have also heard to avoid using the phrases "Thank you" or "I'm sorry" and beware of hidden meanings in the fairy agreements. They are master manipulators and find loopholes in agreements with humans. They have the power to disappear, heal, hypnotize, and cause sickness. They are known to live in caverns, boulder fields, and under lakes. Encounters with these troublemakers have been documented all across the world. King Henry, Lewis and Clark, the Celtics, and many others have all confronted these creatures over the history of time. Santa has elves and if you switch a couple letters in his name, the picture becomes a bit clearer.

In Florida, I interviewed a man who had a similar run in. At my work, we call him the Duck Dynasty guy. He is a lifelong outdoors man who loves fishing and hunting. After Hurricane Michael, he had to live in the forest with his family. They wrapped tarp around the trees and bathed in the river. He said they had many strange occurrences in the forest but felt safe because his family were protected by the forest children.

I asked him what he meant and he told me an experience he had as a child. There was a large mound on the side of his home growing up and he found a small hole in it. He dug with his hand and it opened up to a small tunnel. He climbed down one hall and it broke off into two directions. He took a right and it opened up into a large chamber. He crawled inside and saw something strange in the corner. He thought it was another young boy and approached the shadow. He went to touch its shoulder and it suddenly turned around. The old man said it was an elf, a little green guy like Yoda. He said the gremlin jumped toward an escape pipe while he was desperately sprawling back to the sunlight.

In Sardinia, Italy, explorers found ruins of a dwarf village. It closely resembles the shire from The Hobbit and Lord of the Rings. The civilization was carved into the rocky hillsides. There are extensive cave systems that have living quarters, ledges, balconies and many other aspects of a sustainable village. This small species of people have played a pivotal role in Greek and Norse mythology.

The Keebler Elves, Gremlins, Critters, the North Pole, leprechauns and Tinker Bell are just a couple of examples of how these little creatures have already crept into our lives. Many people who suffer from sleep paralysis have reported these creatures perching up on their chest and watching them. The victim's mind is awake but the body is asleep. The creature can sense or create this phenomenon. The person is paralyzed with their eyes open forced to look the sleep demon in the eyes. I fell victim to this when I had my tonsils and adenoids surgery when I was younger.

I miss our trailer at Tappan Lake and hope to visit the beaver dam when I'm back in the Buckeye State. I will be ready for anything and well equipped with weapons and shiny gifts. I will have the iron in the bag for emergencies. I'd love to get in touch with Max and catch up. We could go mushroom hunting and fishing. I'm bummed our place got destroyed but I do not think it was personal. I doubt it was the faeries and would let them have the victory if it was. I do not want war and I'm sure I was on their land anyway. Though I do think it was just some scumbag humans, the true monster among us.

CHAPTER 6
BIG SHOW AT THE AGORA BALLROOM

CLEVELAND, OHIO

On stage at the famous Agora Ballroom

The Agora Theatre is the most famous stage in Cleveland. With footprints from Kurt Cobain, Elvis and The Beatles, the ballroom is rich in history. Meatloaf, Iggy Pop and many others enjoyed partying with Hank Laconti, the club's owner, who passed away years ago but has been spotted recently by guests. After a fire, the Agora moved to the 5000 Euclid Block which had a history of its own. Performers and fans alike have experienced supernatural phenomena in this sacred theatre, the haven of guardians.

I've had many good night's at Agora. I saw shows with my dad as a kid and was lucky enough to see Kid Cudi before he blew up. I spent a lot of time in the Lava Room studio next door and was part of a rap group's entourage on the garage stage. On December 15, my group, *The Overlooked Youth,* opened up for Caskey and Stevie Stone on the main stage and all of our lives were forever changed.

After I moved back home from Bowling Green, I started a hip hop group called The Overlooked Youth. It was AllTheHipe, Campaign, Trell, Ding, Dub and I making music and going on adventures. We recorded hundreds of songs in my basement and even went out to BG to visit the studio with Longz. But when we were booked to perform at the Agora, it all became real.

Dubs and I picked up our tickets at Peabody's the week before it was demolished. We needed to sell at least ten tickets to get the slot to perform. Tickets were ten dollars each and we got to keep two dollars of every sale we made. For the real hip hop heads, a Caskey, Stevie Stone Strange Music show would be a no brainer but most people are fair weather. Luckily we sold twenty-seven tickets and got the slot!

I had many dreams about the show approaching the date. The stakes were always so high and everything was in super high definition. I remember one concert being performed on a cliffside and I was having trouble locating the group. Another the parking garage elevators were broken and we were forced to take the fire escape. Then it collapsed and we all died. My mind was going crazy. It's all still in my notebook and I still don't like iron grates.

All the Hipe rolled through and scooped Bird and I up. We stopped at Giant Eagle and picked up some liquor and snacks. We took 71 North and plugged the Agora into the GPS. I coordinated with the crew and called the venue to make sure everything was in line. It was and we arrived to the squad already having a little party in the snow in the parking lot.

We cracked open the bottles to calm our nerves and for the much needed blanket in the blizzard conditions. A few blunts were sparked and we broke out a quick freestyle cypher to get loose. AllTheHipe and I even filmed a music video for, "All Good" but strangely it must have never saved completely due to the cold. Sad because it was a sick vibe outside with the brick and snow.

After a while, we went into the venue to check in

with management and see what stage we were performing on. We dropped off our bags and the boys took to the stage. I went to the back room to turn the rest of our unsold tickets into staff. To my surprise, Caskey was chilling on the couch and I dapped him up. I told him I was the guy who reached out to him that was born the same exact day as him. He remembered and it was a cool moment.

He wished me luck and took off with his crew. The staff invited me in and were happy to see we reached our ticket quota. They let me know we sold the most tickets of all the openers and would be the final act before the headliners. That was exciting news. I was hyped and went back to tell the boys. Again I jumped in surprise when I saw something unexpectedly on the couch. It wasn't a rapper, it was a man in a raincoat. He just stared at me as I ran passed.

The boys were excited to hear the good news but were already smiling because they had just ran into Caskey and Stevie Stone. We gave them a mixture and now had a couple hours to kill before the show. That's when Campaign said we can go to his house. He lived in Lakewood, right next to St.Eds High school, where my dad graduated. We took two cars full of people and essentials and rolled right up to the small apartment.

We listened to our music and basically had a full rehearsal. It was a blast. We all collapsed to the carpet and then Campaign's famous raw papers went into rotation. They asked me if I was more nervous for this show or the one at the rec center years back. I smiled and laughed "Definitely that one, people were threatening to jump me and take over the show. I had to get personal security!" I was definitely a little nervous for this show, but only because my dad was going to be there.

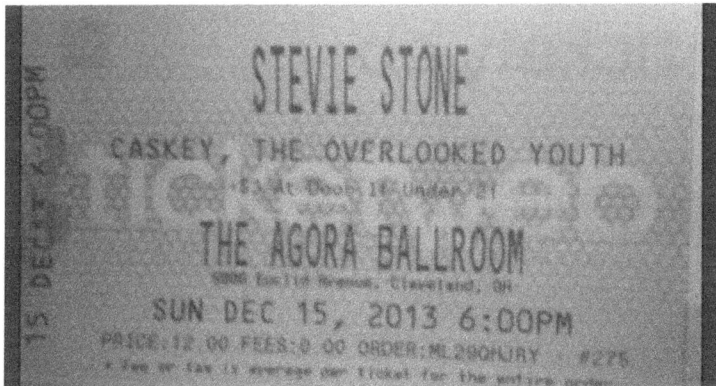

Ticket stub for our show

Someone asked Campaign about his UFO abducting cow tattoo and he explained he has had a couple encounters. Then pointed to me and said two of them were with this guy. Then I laughed and said well I think only one was aliens, the other was Bigfoot.

I put on the song that was inspired by the encounters and the lyrics went:

"It's dark out but the mood's right. Sparking kush blowing smoke in the moonlight. Hear sounds in the woods but it's all good, coz I'm doing what we should, and the moods are right."

We all had our head bobbin and then I said, "But none of that touches doing acid and watching Enter the Void!"

Before we knew it, it was time to go and we were all piling back into the car. As I closed the door, I saw a Vietnam Soldier walking in the distance toward the school. That was more warm than chilling because I knew it was from the story I heard many years as a boy. An Eagle got shipped out to war and his body didn't come back, but his spirit did. The soul always prevails.

We pulled up to the venue and the parking lot was filled. The place definitely had a new feel to it. I was excited to see whose faces were waiting to surprise us inside. ZachDubs and Trell both had big groups that came for them. I was happy to have my dad, Adam and Bird in the crowd supporting. I really wish one of them got a little bit of footage for me.

The opening acts flew by and we were on deck. More and more people flooded toward the stage as we all elbowed each other laughing. We talked to the DJ and then climbed behind the dark curtain awaiting our turn.

My heart was pounding and my knees were trembling but I knew I was exactly where I needed to be.

This adrenaline pumping through my body was what all the hours in the basement were meant for. I closed my eyes and channeled all the artists that foot printed the Agora Stage. I heard Mr. Marley say, "One love, One Heart." Ziggy Stardust advised, "Add water, and just stir." And Kurt told me that the "biggest crime is faking it." I had to go out there and just continue walking my path.

We walked out on stage to a large cheer from the crowd. The drunk fans just copied our close friends who were going crazy. It was definitely working. We signaled to the DJ and when the music dropped, the place exploded. We had them hooked. We had catchy choruses and a wide variety of spitters, a rap fan's dream.

We opened with our squad anthem, *"For My Crew"*, and had most of the fans impressed. They were even singing along to the hook near the end of the song. The lights were so bright that it was hard to see into the crowd. I just stared into the back and performed to the old posters on the wall. I couldn't believe my eyes when they began to come alive.

The song ended and I passed my microphone to Tell so he could perform "Geek Mode " I was on the outro of the song but was so out of it that I let ZachDubs sing the part. I wasn't too worried about it. I still had one more track in between until my song "Monumental" Trell killed it and AllTheHipe was up next with his single "Don't Hate" He stunned the crowd with his opening line "Rollin green on the bible", but definitely had their attention with his cool flow and wise wordplay.

Finally it was time for the finale and the mic was in my hands. I had no choice but to embrace the shadows and pour my heart out. I moved around a lot and really got into the performance. The crowd was vibing along to:

"Grinding til we shine ohh, in it til we do yo, doing what we do until we do it monumental... monumental, monumental. Doing what we do until we do it is monumental."

The entire floor was getting lit and I was really feeling it. I endured the ghosts and actually saw they were rocking with me. They were moving on the walls and some even took to the smoke above the crowd. The lights were still bothering me but I was able to finally look down. I saw beautiful women, hardcore gangsters and dirty punks getting down. Caskey was watching from the back and showed respect.

It felt like a blur and we dropped the mic while the lights went out. We all giggled like schoolgirls on the side of the stage behind the curtain. We were all relieved to just survive the show. We were proud of ourselves.

Creatives from our city never garnished much respect so our small step felt like a truly giant leap.

I gave my dad a hug and dapped up the boys. We were in the books forever. Same stage as some of the greatest to ever do it. We did it ourselves and nobody could ever take it from us. We came a long way from Bonnybrook and Cross Creek but still had a long way to go.

We watched Caskey take the crowd to the next level and even got a shout out from him on stage. I smiled and felt a pat on my back. I looked and saw the man in the raincoat again. I nodded and offered up my hand. When I looked up, he was gone but I knew I had won over his respect and that was enough for me. I rode home feeling like a new man. What a magical night.

CHAPTER 7
THE FAMOUS BASEMENT AT
THE SHELTER
DETROIT, MICHIGAN

The Shelter is most famous for Eminem's 8 Mile rap battles but the same basement holds even darker tales. In the heart of Detroit, this block has connections to Harry Houdini's final show, the filming of Tarantino's True Romance, and the rise of the greatest rapper alive. But when your palms are sweaty, knees weak, arms are heavy, make sure to take precaution in the basement of St Andrews because there is a ghost that wants you back upstairs.

It was Thursday, April 28, 2016, and we were heading to Detroit to see our favorite band. It was the first time I was going to see Sticky Fingers live! They were opening up for Rusted Root who is famous for their song "On My Way". The show was at the St. Andrews Music Hall which was more famous for the basement, "The Shelter".

Dizza in The Shelter basement

Bird came through in the morning and we waited for the girls to pick us up. Bird's cousin Peri and her friend Merissa both saw the boys in Cincinnati a few years earlier and got to hang out with the band after the show. We were excited to have an "in" and some fans as big as us cruising along. The girls were driving and providing the hotel room so we had no complaints. We were planning on sleeping in the car before we linked with them.

Around noon, the girls picked us up and we were westbound! We sang along to *"Bootleg Rascal"*, *"Liquorlip Loaded Gun"*, and *"Australia Street"*. We talked about Lyall Moloney, Taras, and their Queen City show. We all were sad discussing Laika and how the Russians should have never sent her up to space. It was refreshing to bond over the band for all of us. Time flew and we were already at the hotel. That was the quickest two and a half hours I've ever spent in the backseat.

We pulled up to the hotel and had a few hours to kill before the show. Bird walked to the gas station to get drinks and the girls got ready in the bathroom. I laid on the bed and flipped through the channels. I stopped on Brick Mansions. It was filmed here in Detroit and had Paul Walker in it. He battled RZA in a dystopian D-Town and had to save the city from the evil elite. Right up my alley.

Jake came in with both hands full. I smiled but wasn't excited for the alcohol. I was two years sober. But I was ready to smoke one so he poured up and we went outside. We journeyed the nearby area while blazing and were just so stoked for the show. Bird hit me in my arm and said, "The Shelter. Hip Hop history bro." I told him we were gonna have to freestyle down in the basement for old times sake.

We finished the joint and went back to the room. We snuck in and the girls came out minutes later, surprised to see us. They were ready to roll but wanted to pound some quick drinks. Guess I was driving...

Twenty minutes later we were heading to the Shelter. The girls were in the backseat singing when they yelled to turn the music down. They showed us a video that the band just posted. It was Paddy, the bassist, passed out struggling to stand up and talk. Now we were worried if the show was going to be cancelled. What was going on?

I bobbed and weaved through D Town traffic and we had finally arrived. We parked in a sketchy parking lot and paid some homeless guy ten bucks for a piece of paper. We walked past the Garrick Theatre and I told the girls about Harry Houdini's final show.

It was October 24, and he had a 105° fever and cold chills. Houdini was suffering from appendicitis and the toxins were spreading through his bloodstream. When the curtain closed, he collapsed and was rushed to the hospital. He died a week later on All Hallows Eve. Followers still hold a seance on the night of Halloween to communicate with the wizard.

After the magic fun, it was time for some music! There it was, St. Andrews Hall and the famous basement where Eminem got booed off stage and later redeemed himself! The mixture of excitement of the historic location and seeing my favorite band sent me into a psychedelic trance. We followed the girls as they went straight on their mission.

We were told the band was downstairs and my eyes lit up. Sticky Fingers and The Shelter, I felt like I was in heaven. We saw Seamus and he saw the girls. He welcomed them with open arms and we followed right behind. Riss and Peri went around the room like they were reunited with old lost friends. We dapped up the guys and saw Paddy still looking a little rough. Then my phone rang.

It was Bird's uncle, Joe, and he said he was walking toward the venue! Bird and Peri surprised us! We had no idea that their aunt and uncle aka Wednesday Sky was making the trip to D Town. I ran up the steps and ushered them down to the backstage basement. Joe is an old school rock n' rolla, flat earther, and helluva dad. He has been in many bands and played shows across the nation. He saw Paddy and knew right what he needed.

A few minutes later, Paddy was on the couch with me in a headlock! It was awesome! The guys from Bootleg Rascal joined into the fun and the small basement room was rocking. We smoked a few joints and heard a knock on the door. All of us shut up and had that look on our face. I crept over to the door, made sure all the illegal stuff was put away, and opened it expecting to see a cop. There was nobody!

I shut the door and just as we were turning the music back on, another knock. We repeated our paranoid stare as I inched back to the door. But before I could open it, it was one of the venue staff telling us that it was show-time. We asked if he just knocked and he laughed and said no. He knew just exactly what it was.

We stumbled up the steps and fought our way to the front of the crowd. Bootleg Rascal played, *"Overflow"* *"Psychotica"* and my favorite *"Asleep in the Machine"*. The music video is similar to being stuck in the Matrix. Bird and I were the rare few that knew the words and the band appreciated us vibing out.

Next up was Sticky Fingers! We could tell Paddy was still struggling but he was putting on a good mask. The band rocked out and performed "Bootleg Rascal" and all of the other songs that we were singing out in the car. We vibed with the other "Stickies" and even converted a couple Rusted Root fans. The crowd enjoyed the set and demanded an encore. I wanted about ten!

After the show, we hit up the merch tables. The girls wanted new shirts and I was looking for cheap stickers and pins! The boys packed their stuff into the tour bus and came back to the bar. I told Seamus I loved the Guy Ritchie Snatch vibes out "Outcast at Last". Then I ran into

Paddy and asked him how he was doing. He was great and in high spirits.

Two girls approached us and we started chopping it up. We talked about the show and where they were from. They traveled from Chicago. I asked them if they knew that 8 Mile was filmed here and they were stunned. Paddy was surprised too, he caught wind of it but had such a crazy day. He asked me if I wanted a shot and I replied make it a double.

We talked about movies, philosophies and what was next for the band. It was like catching up with a long lost brother. My clone from down under... pause. We talked for a good half hour and it only felt like a couple minutes. He shook my hand and told me he would remember me. Years later, he stuck to his word.

I couldn't find any of my people so I headed to the place that I knew best. By now, the security was treating us like we were part of the band. We felt like we owned the place. I pulled the curtain open and saw some familiar faces. It was all my friends with Dizza, the lead singer. I hopped right in the rotation and told Dylan that he killed the show. He thanked me and passed me the joint.

Uncle Joe and Dylan chopped it up about guitar stories. Bird and I were still in amazement from the entire night while the girls had their hearts set on one thing. We were living characters from the rock n roll fantasy stories that were told in Almost Famous and Pirate Radio!

Dylan previewed us some music. We got to hear "Flight 101" long before it was released! But even more exciting, we started freestyling. I recorded the audio and put it on YouTube! It was one of the best moments in my musical career and it was spontaneously down in the basement Shelter. How fitting. The clip has almost eight thousand views now and gives the Sticky fans a taste of the Frostman's hip hop stoka side.

Another knock on the door, but by now we didn't care. One of the staff came in with a bucket of drinks and told us it was on the house. We were swallowed up by the vibes and I think our party was louder than the stage upstairs. Dylan, Joe and Bird did a pull up contest on the rafters and I was standing on the table videotaping. It was a blast. True rock n roll. But now I had to go to the bathroom!

I fumbled out of the room and followed the wall to the bathroom. The lyrics from "Lose Yourself" played in my head. This was the same bathroom that B Rabbit was puking up his mom's spaghetti. I bobbed my head, rapping while using the restroom. I felt a cold chill down my spine and then my head jerked back. Something pushed me hard right below my neck. I slammed into the wall, falling off balance, peeing on myself, yelling, "WTF!"

I expected to see Bird or maybe even one of the band mates behind me but there was nothing. I walked out and searched the entire basement. I hopped the barricade and checked out the Shelter floor. There was a weird feeling in the air and I could feel a small rumble beneath my feet. I was stuck in a confused daze when I heard yelling coming from the hallway. It was the staff asking me what the hell I was doing.

I made my way to the backstage room and they all asked me where I had been. I questioned them if they were messing with me in the bathroom and they looked just as confused as I did. The staff followed me in and said the venue was closing soon and we would have to make our way outside. I took a sick picture of Dizza doing a handstand up front of the famous 313 graffiti wall before heading out.

The girls followed Dylan onto the bus so we went down the street to a bar to kill some time. We marveled over the show and drank some water to sober up. Venue staff was there for a late night drink and said that was one of the best shows in recent time. I asked them if paranormal activity was common at the venue. And all three of the staff nodded yes. They said there were reports of shadow figures, loud bangs, and electronic issues. I explained what happened to me and they told me I was not the first person to be assaulted in the bathroom.

We got a text from the girls asking them to pick them up in the morning. We said goodbye to Wednesday Sky and decided to walk around the city for a bit. It was a beautiful night and I wanted to make sure I was good to drive since it wasn't my car and I was out of state. We wandered around the eerie concrete jungle, past the behemoth Guardian Building to the Masonic Temple. It was haunting, no wonder why Gosling chose it for the cover of "Lost River".

Luckily we made it to the hotel safely. We sat outside and smoked a joint contemplating if the night actually happened or not. We were stuck in amazement. After a while, we decided to retire at night and go up to the room. When we first walked through the door, the hallway reminded us over the Overlook. There was a thick feel to the air so we took a picture down the hallway. It was very eerily looking.

We passed out and somehow our phones died while on the charger. We overslept and the girls had to get dropped off at the hotel. They were pissed but it was a great night. I wonder if they heard any strange sounds sleeping outside The Shelter, I'm sure the rest of the band did! Keep your eyes peeled for spectres and spectrals while in the land of tigers, lions and pistons or your wings might be red...or dead.

CHAPTER 8
SQUIRE BOONE CAVERNS
MAUCKPORT, INDIANA

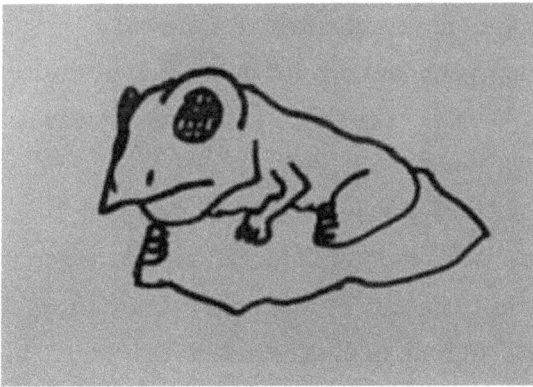

The Eye of the Frog

T he Squire Boone caverns and mill are one of the most historic locations in the state of Indiana. The cave is filled with underwater streams, beautiful stalactites and stalagmites, and very rare underground waterfalls. Squire, the younger brother of

Daniel Boone, cc the 18 foot wheel and grist outside of the cavern.

Squire Boone discovered the system while escaping pursuing Indians and considered it holy ground. His four sons buried Squire in the cavern and sealed the entrance behind him but many people believe he still explores his favorite cave. There have been sightings of him and other

The cool families from our baseball team were looking for some off the radar tourism while visiting Louisville. We already went to the Louisville Slugger Bat Factory and the minor league Louisville Bats baseball game but were looking for more adventure. I recommended Waverly Hills Sanitarium but that was quickly dismissed.

I looked at the pile of hotel coupon flyers that I picked up and a light bulb turned on. We had to go to the caves! The mega cavern was either closed or all reserved so we had to find an alternate. My dad found the Squire Boone caves and we were westbound across the Ohio River and into Indiana.

As we crossed the water, my mom told us about the Ohio River Monster. The creature looked like the creature from black lagoon and a praying mantis. In the fifties, a father son duo was fishing early in the morning and were chased out of a creek by a green slime covered monster. Another girl was pulled underwater and was left with a green stained bruise. After the incident they deemed it the Green Clawed Beast. There have been hundreds of encounters reported. Mom and I may have encountered two of the creatures one morning fishing at Cats Run.

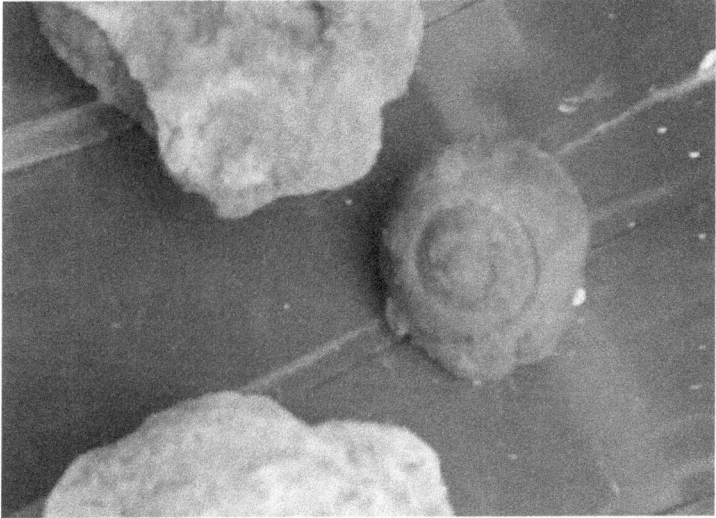

Cavern fossils

There have also been many Bigfoot and dogman sightings near the water as well. In 1994, along the river audio was recorded of a Sasquatch yelling in Wellsville. These calls are known as the Ohio Howls. There have also been many giant bones excavated in the Ohio Valley and that is stone cold proof that we are not the alpha of the pyramid.

We arrived at the caverns and it was a true sanctuary.

The giant wheel and grist immediately caught our attention as we herded towards it. We learned about the history and wildlife of the region. It reminded my mom of her parents' farm in southern Ohio. They went over the cavern rules and regulations and we were ready to go.

As we descended underground, my third eye was tingling. Each twist and turn was mesmerizing to the eyes but even deeper on a spiritual level. The country's largest rim stone dam waterfall back lit with neon lights sent my senses into overdrive. Everyone in our group was speechless. We had no choice but to soak all of the 54° experience all the way up.

As we moved forward on the tour, I began to feel uneasy. I felt like something was watching us. I tried to wedge myself in the middle of our group. I tried to focus on the shadows without letting them know I noticed them. Every new angle had a drop off and hidden tunnel that I could have just been pulled into. I was nervous. Sweating and my glasses were fogging up. I closed my eyes and called to Squire to look after me.

As I continued, I noticed hundreds of frogs staring me down. Everywhere I looked I could feel their eyes checking me out. I felt like they were reporting back to a higher being... I tried to tell myself that it was the spirit of Squire but the legend of cave dwelling reptilians and Loveland Frogmen flooded my anxiety. I paced forward just not trying to fall down a deep crevice into the preda-tor's trap. Then finally a gift from the good, I heard a call that the grave was up ahead.

We approached his grave and the uneasiness was dissolving. The boulder was lifted and I had Squire to thank. I'm not sure what force was following me but it just caught me off guard. I wasn't prepared. I learned real quick that the caverns were not Sea World, not Disney-Land. They were the home of the unknown. Designed by the creators fingerprint and still unexplored by man. When I'm twenty-one grams , I'll have Squire give me the tour.

CHAPTER 9
OHIO RIVER MONSTERS
POWHATAN POINT, OHIO

The Green Clawed Beast

The Ohio Valley region is full of many mysteries and monsters. Excavations have uncovered giant skeletons, mammoth bones and piles of hidden treasure. Haunted prisons and abandoned homes razed the area. Giant catfish and the green clawed beast patrol the waters while the Mothman navigates the sky.

In the late sixties, many locals encountered the Bird-man. Witnesses claimed they have seen a creature with a twelve foot wingspan and giant red eyes. The phenomenon swept the valley and the mothman fever was spreading. Many claimed the animal was a thunder-bird, a pterodactyl that survived the Ice Age. Others claimed it was a screeching owl and a very bad omen for the town.

Tragically in Point Pleasant, the Silver Bridge collapsed and many people died. Some townspeople blamed the winged beast while others claimed that he was trying to warn them. After the accident, many people labeled the creature as a demon. The Devil's crossroads and valley curse theories gained traction after the grieving locals searched for any explanation of why all this was happening.

I believe the creature was flesh and blood. There have been sightings of similar creatures all around the world. The Garuda is very popular in Indian culture. The mothman could have been a dragon or gargoyle breed creature. The descriptions remind me of the monster in Jeepers Creepers and Darkness Falls.

If this creature exists, they are surely masters of their environment. They would be able to manipulate vibra-tion and sound. The animal would most likely have eyes of an eagle and sonar ability like bats. The being may be able to use infrasound and even telepathy. The Mothman Prophecies movie and book both painted interesting pictures of phenomenon that took place in Point Pleasant.

River trout from the Ohio River

We grew up hunting and fishing along the Ohio River. There was a road and creek called Cats Run that we would follow to the river. We used to visit my grandpa's best friend Denzel and hit up the local junkyard for parts all the time. There were plenty of deer, coyotes, and running dogs.

It was a narrow bumpy ride. Sometimes it would get flooded out and others boulders would landslide down and block the road. It was dangerous but secluded. I used to drive the car down there when I was eleven. My dad's best friend from three hours away has family on this little run. Crazy. Everything is connected.

PeePaw would set up mini traps and we would stop by and fill up on bait on our way down. Sometimes there were snakes that would get up in the cage and eat all the minnows. They'd drown but it was still startling when u lifted the cage out and saw a large serpent head. PePa would always make me get deep in the fishing holes. I always hopped back and scanned the region with my eyes wide. The bigger ones couldn't even fit in those traps.

Those were some of our favorite swimming holes. I found some awesome fossils of leaves down there. The rock is about a foot long. It was surreal finding it. It didn't look real as I peered through the water. I picked it up and couldn't believe my eyes. Just like the time we watched an ostrich trample through the woods above us. They escaped from a local farm and had a kill order on their heads. They were very aggressive. Cats Run was crazy.

But one morning after getting our minnows down Cats Run. We were fishing near the mouth of the river and creek where there were some steep cliffs and untouched water. It was hard to reach but pristine territory if you were able to fish it. My grandpa loaded up the equipment while I ran past my mom and climbed over a ledge.

I scanned for fish and in the distance, I saw two giants with their backs out of the water. They were green colored and had spikes coming from them. I pointed and called out. At first glance, I thought they were big catfish but it just didn't add up. They were much bigger than me. And I know big cats have strange fins but these looked more lizard like. I watched the large shadows swim off back into the creek.

This was some kind of serpent. It could have been a large horned snake or a pair of them. Part of me wanted to say it was a crocodile or alligator but I knew they weren't really in these waters. It truly reminded me of the creature from black lagoon. The location and even the gillman creature were so similar. PePa and my mom definitely sensed something strange in the air but sadly never got a visual. I saw them arch out of the water like a dolphin swimming.

There have been reports of a father and son seeing a mantis-like creature covered in slime while fishing. In Kentucky a lady got pulled underwater and scratched by "the green clawed beast". She had a green stain on her leg for weeks. Some people connected it to the Loveland frogmen and aliens.

In the 1800s, they hunted a giant snake in Cincy Valley. They found one that was 24 feet long and many legends of Wendigo along the river. A translucent biped with no nose. Sharp teeth and piercing eyes. That climbs in the trees... there's more than 10 different monsters of towns along the river.

I've also heard many reports of catfish the size of Volkswagen beetles that hang out by the coal barges along with bull sharks, paddlefish, and giant eels. The contaminated water holds many secrets. Bigfoot and ufo encounters are prominent in the valley. Tunnels to middle earth are rumored to be nearby. The weight of these secrets might be heavier than we understand. Moundsville Prison and burial mounds of giants are along the curvy water for a reason.

I'm not sure what the species I spotted that morning but it surely fueled my spirit for fishing and hunting the unknown. The river bank has changed shape and terrain over the years but the creatures would have to go some-where. I hope they are able to find a deep den some-where in the woods where they won't be bothered. I'm sure other fishermen in Cats Run have spotted the same beasts. The family tree would have to be pretty large by now. I hope so.

CHAPTER 10
SMOKE AT THE MUSEUM
WASHINGTON DC

Flag bearer. Eighth grade trip to the nation's
capital.

The Museum is full of American and human history. There is no surprise that some of the collection still has some life in it. Night watchmen have reported hearing sounds and witnessing strange occurrences during late hours. In the zoo, ghosts have been spotted watching Shantai, the Asian elephant. Night at the Museum may have some stronger roots in reality than we first thought.

On our eighth grade school trip, we went to Washington DC! The entire year we learned about the places and people we would encounter on our journey. We learned about the White House, the statues and monuments, and of course the museums! We watched movies and did presentations to be well versed in the way the District of Columbia operates. Well, I had straight A's in the classroom and was pretty street smart but I was not prepared for what I came across in the palace.

My parents dropped me off early in the morning and we gathered in the homeroom eagerly awaiting our departure. Sal's aunt was our history teacher and our chaperone for the trip. She was very passionate about what she taught and I really appreciate that now looking back. She always had fun interesting facts because she cared enough to dive deep into it and level with us. But she was strict, no doubt about that!

The time was here and we climbed onto the bus. This was no yellow school bus, they were fancy greyhound type buses with reclining seats. We got to eat snacks and watch National Treasure during the seven hour drive. We drove through the Shawnee State Park in Pennsylvania. The region provided refuge for Native Americans on their migration from Potomac. The Allegheny Mountains were abundant in UFO and Bigfoot sightings and encounters.

As Nic Cage was stealing the Declaration of Independence, we crossed into Virginia. I felt a little closer to my Aunt Claire and Uncle Joe who I visited a few times as a young boy in Baltimore. We cruised the winding turnpike and stopped for a break between the South Mountain and Greenbrier State Parks.

As others used the restroom, I investigated. I remembered learning about the battle that occurred here that took nearly five thousand lives. I saw an older man that looked like a hunter. I approached him and asked him if he had ever seen any ghost in the hills. He shook his head no but said he had seen the abominable snowman. The hunter claimed many people had seen the tan Sasquatch. I was electrified!

I hurried back on the bus and was glued to the window. We took off east and that was the last stop before we reached DC. We settled at the hotel and got our itinerary plans for the week. We had a busy schedule with stops at the popular spots around town but I was most excited to see the Museum.

That night we were all restless. We watched Dwayne Wade and the Miami Heat win the NBA championship, played poker and wrestled each other. We called them "Challenges". We had piles of junk food and told scary stories all night. Kilbane said that there was a base underneath the District of Columbia and the government has a secret treaty with aliens. Sal said we were bound to run into the illuminati and Bird reminded me of what I needed to hear. He said, "I heard the museum has giant bones!"

The next morning, I was up early but feeling the effects from the night before. I think we all were. The only choice we had was to keep moving forward. We each chugged a mountain dew and climbed into the bus. Before we knew it, the driver was parking the bus at the most notorious museum in all of the land.

When we finally got inside, we scattered in excitement, running wild checking out as much we could. Then we heard that Dylan and Cole Sprouse were there and everybody flocked towards them! I had a different mission in mind. I went up to a female staff member and asked her if she knew if they had a secret vault or underground chamber for the most important history. She seemed to have no idea what I was talking about and said that everything they had was out on the floor for display.

I linked back up with the guys and they all had stories of their own. Kilbane met up with some Cali girls, Sal got to see Zack and Cody, and Bird was hounding for answers like me. We all marveled at the fossils, automobiles, and fascinating inventions from the timeline of our country.

I felt a nudge in my side and it was Brad. He noticed that some of the workers were following us. We let Bird and Sal know and we knew what we had to do. Instantly we scrambled in all different directions. The workers focused on Bird and I. They must have been upset about our questions. We just wanted to know our true history! It felt like the game Jumanji was coming to life!

Luckily I saw my teacher and made my way towards her. She noticed that I was visually upset. I really feared the workers were going to harm me. I have heard of what they have done to other people digging for answers. I told her that the workers were chasing after us. She asked us if we had stolen it. We of course denied that. After a few minutes, we located Sal and Brad but we could not find Bird.

I was beginning to get nervous that they captured him and were dragging him down to their dungeons. By now he could have been in the tunnels below the White House. I told our teacher that we were asking about giant bones and the ancient tablets that they were hiding. She shook her head and said, "Oh no". She was also very aware of the lengths the museum went to, to keep their agenda afloat.

To our surprise, we finally found Bird. He was sitting on a bench just waiting for someone to locate him. He had a strange look on his face. They must have caught up to him. He was in a trance and wasn't able to explain what happened until we got back to the hotel.

Bird was holding back tears and really struggling. He said the staff had captured him and dragged him to a room in the back. When the door opened up, it was pitch black, a hole to oblivion. Possibly an entrance to the underworld. The men threatened to throw him in there but luckily decided against it. I'm sure it would have been too much blowback, being a kid on a school field trip and all.

CHAPTER 11
OCEAN CITY BOARDWALK
WORCESTER COUNTY, MARYLAND

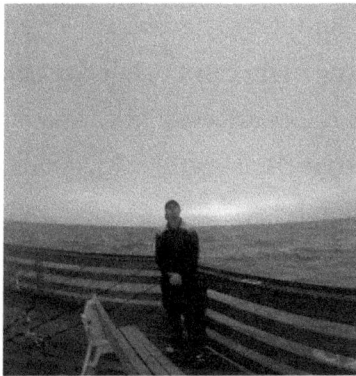

Boardwalk of memories.

he Ocean City boardwalk has received recognition from the Travel Channel, National Geographic and USA Today as one of the nation's best boardwalks. The incredible food, huge variety and positive vibes bring vacationers every year. The Ferris wheel, i and infamous Morbid Manor keep the visitors screaming but the real life haunts of the life saving station and Colored Hotel might linger in the tourist dreams forever.

It was the first vacation with my dad's fiancé and her family. We were heading to Ocean City and I had no clue where it was. But it had to be by a beach, so I was content. My dad and I were excited to snorkel and lounge in the ocean while all the girls were ready to hit the seaside shops. They all were laughing and cackling "No tax in Delaware!"

It was about a seven hour drive and we were all exhausted. We stopped for groceries, unpacked and they all crashed for the night but I needed a little beach action. I walked down the boardwalk and was enthralled by all the sights and sounds. It really came alive at night. There were colored hotels, carnival games, and even a Ferris wheel!

The haunted house caught my eye and I had to check it out. I walked over to it, looking to see what the story was and how much it was. This cool looking rock n roll chick walked over and told me this place used to be cool but she could take me to a real haunted spot. I of course was down for the adventure and followed her.

We didn't walk far and we arrived at the Life Saving Station. Sadly it was closed but we could still peek around. This place was a museum for over 300 ship-wrecks along the coast. I could already feel the air around the building was different. The girl told me that many people have experienced supernatural things in the area. Some hear sailors chattering, a girl playing, and dinner bells ringing.

The girl smiled at me and told me to look inside the window. I didn't know what to look for but really didn't hesitate. I curled my hands up and peeked inside. I scanned the inside and couldn't see much. I repositioned and kept searching the interior. Then I saw something that made my breathing speed up.

Trippy venue mural

It was water on the ground. I followed the puddle and saw boots. I said no way and kept raising my eyes. I couldn't believe my mind. It was a man and he was soaking wet. He was around my age but looked different. He needed help. I ran to the front door and tried to open it. Of course it was locked and I peaked in the window, but I could see nothing. No evidence the water was even there. I circled the building twice again checking every window for a visual or a way in.

The girl knew what I saw. She had seen him before too, many people have. I followed her walking and we turned onto the pier. I wondered how many sharks were within a quarter mile? How many mermaids had sonar on us and how close the nearest treasure chest was and the kraken defending it.

She reached for my hand and I let her grab it. I was holding hands with a complete stranger walking toward oblivion. I was wondering what life is. I was wondering if she was gonna kill me or love me. I didn't know what it was but it felt good. We continued walking in silence and I was just trying to soak in all the vibes. Crashing waves, pretty girl, ghost sailor, and the endless abyss lying ahead.

We stopped at the end of the pier and she let go. She said she had to tell me something. I was all ears. She said she was contemplating suicide tonight before she met me and she didn't expect me to go along on her little journey.

I replied it was no problem and she was a great tour guide while smiling, looking into her eyes. She blushed and said she would be fine tonight but everyday is a struggle. I agreed to give her a hug.

The warmth felt nice and I rubbed her back to comfort her. She whispered in my ear but I could barely hear her. She said, "Storms were coming" I felt that she thought I was a decent person and was trying to look after me. She was warning me of something. We held hands on the way back from the pier and I gave her my number. Sadly I never heard from her again but I am still waiting.

Oddly enough, that pier was destroyed three times by severe storms and hurricanes in the next few years. I hope my bonita boardwalk baby is somewhere happy following her destined path. Maybe it will lead back to me but if not, no worries coz it's meant to be! I'm sure she is walking, changing the tides with every step.

CHAPTER 12
ANNIE PFEIFFER CHAPEL
LAKELAND, FLORIDA

Frank Lloyd Wright masterpiece.

The Annie Pfeiffer Chapel is one of the most beautiful buildings on Florida Southern's campus. It was designed by Frank Lloyd Wright himself and part of his "Child of the Sun" collection. There have been reports of students seeing a ghost of FLW inspecting a choir screen that was installed incorrectly. So next trip out to Lakeland, make sure to visit the magical campus that has mysteries deeper than apparitions.

In 2017, my childhood home sold and it was time to hit the road. I lived with my best friend Adam for and while doing overnight tile and grout work but in January I was set to referee at the USFTL National Championships in Plant City. I took the passenger seat out of my car and after doing a lot of research I was ready to live out of my Ford Contour for a while. I planned to camp at boat docks, state parks, and maybe couch surf if I was lucky.

After a couple nights sleeping behind Walmart, on back roads, and at rest stops, I was beginning to have second thoughts. I was out looking for gators when I got a notification from the couch surfing app. I was accepted to stay at a house of a guy who looked like a surfer and that was totally cool with me. After a while of feeling each other out, he shot me the address and I was on my way. A bit later I drove through the beautiful Florida Southern campus and arrived at my future home.

The first thing I noticed was the bars over the windows. The second was the thousands of lizards scattering through the yard and up the trees. I knocked on the door and had no idea what to expect. A non surfer dude answered the door and said his name was Bass. He said Phil was in the shower and the couple was in their room. There was a drum set, guitars, and inspiring posters all over the walls. It was mesmerizing. Phil came out and said let's adventure!

Finally learning guitar in Lakeland, Florida

I hopped on the bike and followed those two on their longboards. They showed me Mason's Rolling Hills, the Shapeshifter's house, and led me downtown Lakeland. We passed the Polk Theatre, Munn Park, and then circled around Lake Mirror. They showed me the statue of Blinky, the gates under the city, and of course the beautiful Terrace Hotel. I was intoxicated of new vibrations and the entire experience was finally beginning to make sense.

I followed the boys through cool back roads and pulled up on some bright colors and grand architecture. There was music playing, beautiful girls everywhere and just an incredible feeling in the air. This was it, heaven on earth. That exotic Florida college atmosphere us Ohioans dream of while growing up. They both quickly informed me that Frank Lloyd Wright designed the campus and there were many legends throughout these blocks.

We pulled up to the prettiest piece on campus and I was instantly mesmerized by the beauty. The chapel glowed in the sunlight and was surrounded by luscious green bushes and trees. The unique design of shapes and angles was intoxicating. It reeled me right in. We parked our bikes behind shrubs and entered.

Red seats filled the floor and upper deck like the Crimson tide. The building was even bigger inside than I thought it would be and the sun spread through the top glass creating magical rays. We only spent a few minutes there but it felt like hours. The cathedral had an energy within it. I knew I'd be back.

As we grabbed our bikes, they told me the place was haunted. They said Frank Lloyd Wright reveals himself at night as many other spirits wander campus. They saw that I was interested and said that we will do our investigating later. We cruised home and then hopped in the car to explore the city. They showed me Tiger stadium, some nearby lakes, and the Southgate shopping Center, where they filmed Edward Scissorhands! Days went by and we all grew closer. They officially asked me to join the musical and I moved in!

I was living my dream. I was on the ground floor of an original production. The music was killer, the story had twists and turns and there were cool elements like witches and goblets. I was exactly where I needed to be. But all that came at a cost. It was tough being thrown right into a cycle that wasn't slowing down for anyone.

I missed my family, my pets and the home I grew up in. I missed spending nights with my friends watching sports and talking about conspiracies. I missed having a place to call my own. I missed my bed and had shower to myself. I missed peaceful mornings and nights that I got to escape into the moonlight. I missed going in the kitchen and not having to worry about getting glass in my feet. I missed Skyping with my girl and she missed that too.

I was living a strange lifestyle. Going to drag shows and punk rock concerts. We hand made most of our clothing and had spikes and patches decorating the outside. We were up all hours of the night brainstorming for the musical and screen printing for our costumes and merch. We played a lot of Dungeons and Dragons. I lost touch with a lot of friends back home and was beginning to lose myself a bit.

My girlfriend wasn't very patient with the new life change and we were on the rocks. She was in Dallas and I was stuck in the swamps. Some nights I wished I just drove to Texas and started my life there instead of Lakeland. One night she was angry at me and hung out with a group of guys. Tragically, she was drugged and assaulted. She almost lost her mind from the experience and barely could talk to me. I felt so helpless and lost. I just wanted my baby back.

That news hit me like a semi truck. I wasn't expecting all the trauma. I was hurt, betrayed and just sick for her sake. She didn't deserve that, nobody does. I was mad at her but felt guilty myself. I was furious and wanted to kill those guys. They were scum. It still boils my blood. I just needed to get away so I grabbed my bike and just started pedaling.

I sparked a joint and took off toward the college. I was crying and questioning my entire calendar year. Before I moved, the relationship was solid and I truly believed she was my destined soul mate. I understand most connections go through trials and tribulations but being homeless has sent our relationship into a spiral. I was looking for some answers on how to save myself and the relationship.

Fishing Tampa Bay

I parked my bike and sat my back against the chapel while ripping my j. I was wiping the tears and snot from my face when I felt a cool breeze. I continued whimpering when I heard a soft touch on my shoulder. It didn't register at first because I didn't hear anyone approach but then I felt it grasp stronger. I opened my eyes and saw the surrounding area was misty.

Out of the mist, I could hear a voice. They were welcoming me and letting me know that I was safe to be there. The voice wanted me to know that it was all right to let it all out. The emotion just rained out of me. All the pain from the sleepless nights finally found the drain. The angel said the brightest days are after the darkest nights. Our useful tools are an eraser and a wrecking ball. This year has been my deletion and the rest of my life is the blank slate I have to work with.

I walked back toward my bike and could hear music approaching. I recognized the song and knew it was a familiar face. It was Phil. He asked if I wanted to take a lap around Lake Hollingsworth and of course I was down. I loved seeing all take the fancy houses and having the place to ourselves.

I rode no hands and felt so much peace. I would close my eyes and just smile as the wind pressed my face. Then I heard my name yelled urgently. I opened my eyes and swerved off the path. There was a giant ten foot alligator laying right across the cement. That was a super close call.

We got back to the house and met up with our neighbor, Larry "Big" Prine, rest in peace my friend. We always circled around the block, talking about neurolinguistics and the Manson family. He toured the country with Richard Bandler doing seminars on the power of the brain. He was also good friends with Paul Crockett and even visited him on his famous ranch. He knew all the inside information about Manson, Paul Watkins, and Spahn Ranch.

Big thought it was so cool that I was from Ohio like Charlie. He has some incredible shows on the 7 Principles of Huna. I miss drinking beers and rooting on the Dodgers, playing pool. They won the World Series for him the year he passed. I fell asleep to his radio show and the Sun was brighter in the morning. The birds were singing and lizards were roaming. I was rejuvenated.

CHAPTER 13
MY NIGHT AT THE TERRACE
LAKELAND, FLORIDA

Frances Langford Promenade (tunnels under the city?)

The Terrace first opened in 1924 and has watched Lakeland grow up with a front row view. Overlooking Lake Mirror and downtown, the historic hotel sits on Main Street and Massachusetts Avenue not far from the Confederate statues of Munn Park. Visitors enjoy the high ceilings and tropical gardens but some have spotted a ghost of a bride who hung herself the night of the wedding. So next time you visit or see the Terrace, pay extra attention to the fifth floor! Til' death do us part!

My Biltmore roommates were very spiritual. Starting the very first day, we did group meditations. We do a multi step warm up exercise and follow it with a deep meditation. We would do facial stretches, hum in harmony, shoulders to ears, mindlessly chatter, leg and neck stretches and other things to warm our mind and body to enter trance. We also used different crystals, incense, candles, and mists to induce a deeper state of dreamworld.

Next level work included loud screams, curling up into a ball as tight as we could, and holding our breath. We would switch up invoking and lesser banning rituals and try new places like the backyard, near the lakes, and midnight at a cemetery. Overtime we developed strong cohesion and invited others to join our meditations. The group aspect was a multiplier for vibrations. We inherited each other's skills and thrills, similar to the concept of Sense8.

We worshipped to the east at sunrise to Ra, south at noon to Hathoor, west at sunset to Tum and north at midnight to Khephera. We explored opposites like safety & danger, victory & defeat, pleasure & pain, good & evil, u & hell, god & the devil and of course love & death. For about me flames the pentagram and in the column stands the six rated star. We studied chakras, the stars, and many gods from the past.

We kept daily journals on the experiments and worked them into our artwork. We broke glass and dishes in the kitchen to relieve stress and push the boundaries. We made clothing, songs, and jewelry at all hours of the night that connected to our pinnacle project, the musical. We were a family and working machine of many parts. It was one of my favorite teams I have ever played on. It was the hardest I have ever worked and during our sold out shows, I actually felt proud. I watched this project evolve from the ground floor in glass corner. Plus it had themes up my alley with the holy grail, witches, and magical potions! Yes!

One night in February after rehearsal, we invited a couple cast members back to the Biltmore to smoke, meditate and make some music during the Penumbral

Lunar Eclipse. We were all in good spirits, dancing and singing the lyrics to our favorite Days N' Daze songs. After a while we passed around the pipe and some drinks. We were feeling super groovy and ready to meditate our minds and bodies.

The extra bodies and souls in the room were definitely felt. You could feel the new hums entering the chorus. We were midway through the exercise and the vibrations felt amplified by the moon. I watched the candle flicker and it felt like a storm cloud arrived. Moments later, the door burst open and Slash came stumbling in. She had been stabbed. She was bleeding everywhere. The knife was serrated. This is how she got her nickname.

I was still in a trance and was not sure what was happening. It was like a horror movie was unfolding in the hallway while I was laying on the floor in a crouching position tripping out. The vibe went from Buddha to Freddy Krugha as pandemonium erupted. I watched a disturbed Phil grab his bike and escape out the back door.. I grabbed mine and went out the front. They treated the wound and stitched her up while we were gone. The Biltmore was covered in pools of blood.

I went straight to my safe haven. I rode my bike downtown and sat beside Lake Mirror. I had to get that image out of my head. I could see her bone and in my trance I could see every detail. Her blood spurting out painted the picture of how it happened. Her old best friend attacked her because he blamed her for the death of their third best friend. I was sitting next to the Frances Langford Promenade, wondering how deep those tunnels actually go.

After climbing and dangling my feet over the water, I crawled up the hill and sat next to the giant swan statue and lit up a joint. I felt I was finally getting back to normal while gazing at beautiful lights over the lake. My heartbeat was moving towards steady when I heard a soft voice behind me asking if it could join me?

I wiped the tears from my eyes and smiled at the girl, nodding yes. I offered her the smoke but she politely declined and what was wrong? I told her I had been away from home for too long. I just wanted to see a familiar face and I missed my family. A new family accepted me into their home but this one was more dysfunctional than the one back in Ohio.

I didn't even mention the blood but she pointed to my pants and asked, "And that?" I told her our house was the only place the victim could go and the girl realized that there were many elements at play here. She reached over and grabbed my hand, while staring into my eyes, she whispered, "That I deserve a break."

She left me with something cold in my grasp so after a few seconds I looked down and saw an old key in my hand. I thought she was inviting me to her home but when she nodded toward the Terrace, I figured she wanted to hook up. The mystery woman had different plans. She gave me a hug and kissed me on the cheek and started walking in the opposite direction. I was confused and pretty much back in the trance. I cried out "You're not coming?" She confidently said, "I've got a train to catch!"

I was really confused because I knew the last train was around seven but she was out of sight in a couple seconds. I walked over to the Terrace and was enthralled by its luxuriousness. I enjoyed the Victorian design, it reminded me of the Summit Inn near OhioPyle. I didn't know how to explain it to the lady at the front desk and didn't have time to check every door so I was beginning to panic. I continued walking around observing the antiques and photos on the wall. I saw a picture of the old city and I was back in my altered state.

I had walked these halls before, many times actually. It was right after the hotel opened and I was here on business. I had a room on the fifth floor and wore clothes that I never remember purchasing. I was clean cut, tipped the doorman and smoked a cigarette by the lake every morning. There was a baby gator with one eye, I named him Blinky. The sound of the train was soothing in the midnight skies. I laid on my bed, excited for a date that I had with the girl at the front desk at the end of the week when I heard a loud pound at the door.

My eyes opened and I was back in sweatpants with messy hair all in my face. The knock was still at the door but it was faint. I found my glasses and hustled over to the door. I undid both of the locks and opened it. There was nobody there. I searched both sides of the hallway and found nothing but nostalgia.

CHAPTER 14
EXPLORING FORT DESOTO
PINELLAS COUNTY, FL

Clip from music video in Fort Desoto

Fort Desoto was the original home of the buccaneers and some say they still game after dark on the grounds. Many soldiers died during the Spanish American war from Yellow Fever and have been reportedly seen throughout the campgrounds when the sun goes down. The St Pete Keys are filled with luscious inlets and vast wild life but when you step in the bunker of the fort, it makes you feel like you are protecting the mainland yourself.

We woke up early in the morning to Slash pounding on the door. She said we were going on an adventure. Last trip we took with her, we spent the night on a Tampa Bay pier fishing, making music, and curled up in a ball freezing. But she had all the supplies that I needed, so I was in. We were on the road with a joint sparked and screaming along to our favorite Pat the Bunny songs.

We stopped for a quick tour of Plant City. She showed us where she got kicked out of school and other places she got jumped. She hopped that fence to run from those cops and hid in that abandoned building from these gangsters. She had a lot of funny stories. But one had her shook. She pointed to the bleachers and said, "She's still under there." and proceeded to tell us about a girl that she became friends with under the stands. Which turned out to be her only friend at the football game.

She whipped into a driveway and we asked if it was her house and she giggled and said nope. We followed her, sneaking through the back door in confusion. She went straight to the refrigerator and started making drinks. Roxy asked her what the deal was and she said she was "house sitting or whatever". I avoided touching anything because I didn't want my fingerprints anywhere near here. We gulped down our glasses and urged to hit the road.

After twenty painful minutes of paranoia, we pulled out of the mystery house. Once we left the neighborhood, she said that she actually lived next door and was trying to avoid her parents. They were very strict and were completely oblivious to their outlaw daughter. Her neighbors are out of town for most of the year and she takes advantage of the empty sanctuary.

RV road trip ready

Slash was always up to something. Just the week

prior she asked us to go camping. We of course obliged and packed for the forest. To our surprise we pulled off to a state park, the Sunshine Bridge Fishing Pier State Park! We spent the night on the haunted bridge and had quite the wild time.

We caught plenty of fish and wrote many songs. I filmed a music video and went exploring for a couple hours by myself. I met some shark fisherman and a man who seemed to be living on the pier. He knew all the instructions and outs of the place. We shared a joint and he took me on a little tour. He told me about the tragedy that struck when a boat hit the bridge and caused it to collapse into the sea, killing 40 people. He told me about the 200 people that have jumped to their death. He asked me if I had seen The Punisher and at that time I had realized that it was the bridge from the movie.

I was rambling on when he shushed me and pointed out toward the tall bridge. We both witnessed a shadow figure leap into the water below. I was freaking out, flustered, wondering why he was so calm. He said, "Don't worry, she jumps every night, she'll be back again tomorrow." He asked to light his cigarette and was off to the next chapter of his story. I waved to him as he saluted off into the darkness. I stumbled back to our camp, rolled up into a ball and caught some z's. Successful camping fishing trip.

We drove through Tampa and enjoyed the views on

the bridge to St. Pete. I enjoyed seeing Tropicana Stadium but was looking for the real devil rays. I always keep my eyes peeled for shark fins and mermaid tails. I'd love to see a whale splash one day. She turned off the music and said we were here, Fort DeSoto.

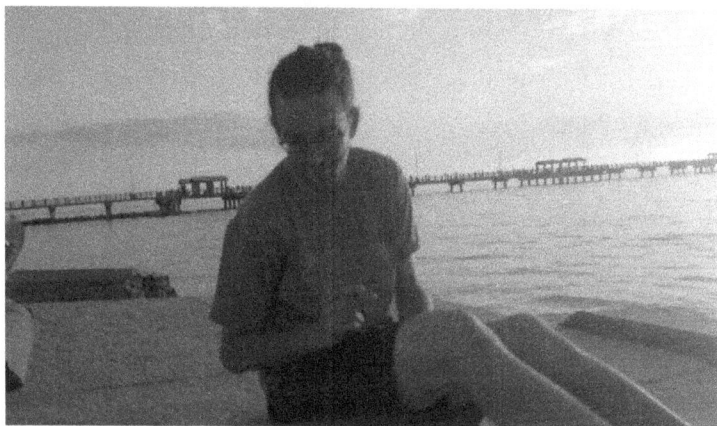

The pier of Fort Desoto

We parked the car and started to follow the lagoon. The coast held surprises at every turn. We saw enormous birds, lizards, and snakes. We even had a close encounter with a manatee. There was a surprising amount of forest and jungle land. We sat on the beach and passed around a spliff. It was a true oasis and we had entertainment, watching the fisherman and boaters. They pulled in nets full of fish and crab.

Time passed and I felt a nudge on my shoulder. I figured we lit another one up and I was holding up the rotation. I opened my eyes and started to mumble something. Slash shushed me up and told me to listen. I closed my eyes and waited. I gave it a few seconds and didn't hear anything. At the exact moment I began to speak, we all heard a strange whistle. I thought it was the gillman but Bass said that was an Indian call. He said the Tocobaga Tribe used to roam here until they were killed by yellow fever and the Spanish invaders. Slash gave a whistle back but Roxy was not having any of that and forced us to get the heck out of there.

But what Roxy didn't know is that we were heading straight to the actual fort and the area of the highest paranormal activity. It still took a while hiking through the forest and that lingering feeling of being watched was still upon us. Finally there it was, the fort! We explored the ginormous mortars and climbed into the bunkers. Bass did the Halo theme song and it sounded incredible reverberating in my chest. We took pictures and had a moment of silence to soak it all in.

During the quiet time, I felt a strong electricity in my chest and a call from the other room. When I opened my eyes,I could no longer see my friends. And when I tried to call out for them, my voice wouldn't work. My heart rate doubled and I began to be very dizzy. I almost fell over when I felt a strong pull on my shoulder. It was Slash asking how the hell I got all the way up on top of the fort. I had no answers and just wanted to sit down.

We followed her to the beach and sat on some of the remnants of the fort. It was quite magical. I filmed a music video while we watched the sun set. After I was done, I sat with my feet dangling watching the waves and the pier. Many unique vibrations are flowing through the fort and some are quite intoxicating. I closed my eyes and rode the roller coaster of the timeline. We all did. It was the cleanse we all needed. Before we left, I grabbed a piece of the fort and will forever cherish it. Man what I'd give to have Slash wake us up for just one more adventure...

CHAPTER 15

HELL WEEK AT THE POLK THEATRE

LAKELAND, FLORIDA

Eight legged freaks

The Polk Theatre has been the subject of many ghost shows over the years but the walls are most famous for housing Elvis Presley. The Lakeland cornerstone has live performances and classic movie nights but the real show goes down after the doors are closed. Ghosts of former employees and performers have been spotted by theatre visitors and even caught on camera. Reality and fantasy blur together in more than just the shows at this box office.

My favorite time of the year is the Halloween vibes of October. I enjoy the scary movies and spooky creativity that spikes in the community. So when I was working as a stagehand on the Rocky Horror Picture Show shadow cast Halloween special at the Polk Theatre, I knew I was in the right place. I was surrounded by freaks and people just like me. Everyone was dressed crazy and so passionate about what they were doing. It was hard not to be motivated while standing on the famous stage in the legendary cathedral.

It was Hell week. The final week before the show and most of the people were stressing out. The show was a two night extravaganza that the entire community would come out and see. The whole theatre would sell out completely both nights guaranteed. I had heard about this weekend for all ten months that I lived in Lakeland.

I was staying over at Crystal Grove now and while I was away it became the unofficial headquarters of the show. They were screen printing, designing flyers, and using the formula that worked so well for the first musical. The area was pretty dangerous but I was just happy to have a roof over my head and a place to park my car.

But I was constantly peeking out the window and watching the people suspiciously walk by. After a long night of our group brainstorming, all the neighboring houses realized we were the ones that they had to be worrying about.

We had freaks of every size, shape, and color. We blared $uicideBoy$ from the stereo and jammed on our guitars. We rehearsed in the grass and put on shows for the neighborhood. All the dope boys and hoochie mama's were big fans of ours. We grilled burgers and played at the park. All the girls loved talking to the neighbors and smoking cigarettes with them late night when they were all drunk. We were a crazy bunch. It was similar to living the college life all over again.

It was awesome seeing my friends in action on stage. Nate and I marveled over their talent as we hauled different sets and pieces. The show was all business but backstage and in the alley were pure craziness. We were drinking, smoking and enjoying all the extra curricular of showbiz. The aura of the theatre was intoxicating itself. There was a lot of pressure and even more drama but to the fans it looked interwoven perfectly.

Nate and I snuck outside and finished off one of our roaches. We talked about Game of Thrones and Norse Mythology. I helped tattoo the Viking wheel on his arm. Nate'a as big as a warrior and has a very long dark beard. He reminds me of a cross of Ragnar Lothbrok,

Rollo, and Hodor. After he hit the blunt, his eyes widened and he asked "What was that?" I felt the urge to look up and caught a quick glimpse of someone peeking over the ledge of the roof. They were gone in an instant and we heard the name being called by the director.

We rushed to the stage and were directed to help carry one of the actresses off of the stage. She had tripped and hurt her ankle pretty badly. They were all worried that she wouldn't be able to dance let alone walk during the performance. Meanwhile, I was contemplating if it has anything to do with what we had seen on the roof.

I was puzzled. She needed ice. They told me to run downstairs and grab something out of the freezer. I shuffled down the stairs and almost did a backflip right back up the steps when I saw something on the floor that I could not believe. It was a spider. I like spiders, that wasn't the problem.

This arachnid was the size of a small dog and it was definitely well aware of my presence. I froze for what felt like a lifetime staring into the blackness of its hundreds of eyes. Then it darted into the corner of darkness. I took the window of opportunity to hit the freeze chest but there was nothing I could use. I dashed back upstairs and just left immediately.

I rode home in disbelief. I wondered if I was hallucinating. I tried to remember what I had to eat earlier that day. In the past, I've had a few trippy experiences of losing reality when dealing with food poisoning. But I had my usual pb & j on toast in the morning and my cheese quesadillas before rehearsal. I wasn't drunk and the herb wouldn't make me see things that weren't there. It may have just opened the door to seeing what is actually there.

I sat in the car for an hour until the rest of the crew started getting home. They all asked me where I was and if I was feeling alright. I told them I was good, just a bit dizzy. They said they had just the right thing to fix that right back up. After a little bit of that, I was in a talkative mood. I told them what had happened in the basement and that was the reason I went home early.

They were all very interested because they grew up there and had heard of and the legends of the Polk Theatre. They each had their own story. They have witnessed the lights flickering, caught orbs in the background of pictures, and heard whispers from the dark. Nate said he heard a voice call my name when we were smoking outside. I told him that's when things started going south. I knew the place was paranormal but what I saw in the basement was a physical being. A true creature from below.

"Like 8 legged freaks man!", claimed Mason from the kitchen. We laughed and agreed of all places possible, Polk County, Florida would be the one. We considered the spider being suped up on meth or some other cleaning chemicals. I wondered if the ocho had been there since the opening of the venue, or maybe long before. We found reports of spiders the size of pigs in the jungle and deep in desert caves. "It's a ghost spider!" smiled Slash.

The next two days went spectacularly. The opening bands were rocking, the dancers put on a spooky show, and the shadow cast was up there with Tim Curry's performance. The crowd was dressed to impress and also wearing to scare! I met a lot of wild freak shows and really got soaked into it. On night two, I knew all the callouts and had my rice ready to throw. But always in the back of my head lingering was that black eyed creature.

A couple nights later, a group of cast returned to the theatre to see a special showing of The Shining. What a perfect cherry on top of the holiday season. Watching one of the best horror movies of all time in an old haunted theatre in late October was like a dream of mine written in the stars. But for a moment, it turned into a nightmare.

As I crept through the dark theatre to go to the restroom. I felt something enter my head and persuade me to enter the basement. I tried to fight it but I lost control almost instantly. I was being guided through the pitch black perfectly and found myself on the steps. Each stair, I tried to resist. I tried to grip the hand rail and wake myself up. I could see the monster's eyes shining in the dark.

As my foot was about to hit the rock bottom, the creature's fangs raised up. I couldn't see them but I could hear them. Just thirsty to latch on to me like they would a deer in the forest. I remembered Harry and Ron running from Aragog the Acromantula in the forbidden forest. I wish I had the chance but then remembered Hagrid's wise words... "To follow the spiders."

I did just that. I relinquished all fear and just embraced the basement beast. I regained control of my body and stepped slowly toward the creature. It blinked its eyes and dissolved into the darkness. I was beside myself. I had a special bond with this thing and it taught me things that I would have never learned without its help. I crawled back to my seat and finished the movie.

The last night we all spent together was a bonfire at Nate's house. It was a celebration! We played with viking swords and threw tomahawks at targets. We lit sparklers and made marshmallows. A couple of us explored his pond with flashlights looking for gators. We sat on his dock and smoked a joint under the stars listening to the sounds of the forest. He asked me about the basement incident and I told them it was an awakening. Then we heard a roar in the woods and we quickly got our asses back to the barn!

CHAPTER 16
KINDEL LANES
MARIANNA, FLORIDA

The Lanes in their glory.

H ave you ever held the door open for someone that you swear was just walking toward you and then they are nowhere to be found? I was parked at the gas station the other day up front of the air compressor. I was unloading recyclables and a car pulled up, needing to use it. So I ran quickly and started my car and looked out the window as I pulled out. I went to wave when I noticed there was no one in the car and I had an interaction that I could not explain. Mysteries are sometimes down your street!

Kindel Lanes was a staple in the town's community until it was tragically destroyed in Hurricane Michael. Before its untimely demise, the grounds provided batting cages, golf, laser tag and of course bowling to locals. Professional wrestling events, concerts, and birthday parties were held on the property as well. The lanes were a spot for the townspeople to escape the hardships of everyday life and feel like a kid again. The building may be broken but the memories will forever be untouchable.

My sister and I were hired in July to be the first two bartenders of the bowling alley. They had just obtained their liquor license and had ads posted all around town that they were looking to hire someone with bartending experience. Well, I watched my dad bartend hundreds of times and bar back in college once so I figured I was the right choice for the job.

Kindel Lanes was the place to be when the sun went down. People of all ages, colors and sizes heard the Kindel call. Bowling leagues flooded the week nights while birthday parties and church gatherings kept us busy on the weekends. I researched many different drink mixtures and watched hours of bartending training videos. It all paid off when I poured the first legal drink in the establishment's history. I was Robert Redford, a natural!

After a long day of strikes and spares, there is still a lot of work to be done. I had to mop the bathrooms, put the balls on the appropriate racks, turn off the machines, and take out the trash in the back. 75% of the building is pitch black when the customers leave. The alley had a warehouse vibe and was very eerie when I was alone.

I heard many legends about the bowling alley while pouring drinks. Interesting stories about the professional tournaments that were held here, finding love on the lanes, and of course the illegal activity in the parking lot. Cars have been broken into, people have been assaulted and unexplainable sounds have roared from the woods in back.

While closing down, it was very common to hear strange sounds in the back. But after a long shift, I didn't have the energy to get all worked up about it. I was primarily focused on just getting out of there as fast as I could. I knew the place was filled with ghosts but if they weren't helping me with closing, then I didn't have much for them. But one night in the bowling alley changed my life for good.

We had reports of broken glass in the back parking lot. A few angry customers came in and were upset about flat tires. We didn't allow customers to bring bottles outside for that exact reason. My boss sent me outside to sweep it up and to try to calm the peace. I didn't mind the task, time flew by while I was out exploring.

The angry customers were gone but I found the pile of broken beer bottles. As I was sweeping up, I heard some shuffling toward the tree line. I figured I just spooked a deer and didn't pay much attention to it. Then I could have sworn I heard someone call my name. I stepped towards it but the sky seemed to get darker. I trusted my sixth sense and took that as a warning. The presence was too intimidating. I had no plans to meet a wild pangoro today.

A few weeks later in October, Category 5 Hurricane Michael made landfall and destroyed the bowling alley. There is a documentary called "Spirits in the Storm" that explores the supernatural aspects of the event. More than sixty people were killed by Michael and thousands were suffering physically, emotionally, physically, financially, and spiritually. We are still in an everyday battle of regaining the balance in this region.

I was personally traumatized by October 11. I was forced to evacuate my trailer and luckily was able to go to my mom's cabin or else I would have been forced to go to the school for public shelter. Over there, we watched the eye of the storm hover above us. After mass destruction, the few minutes of peace were serenity until rampage approached again. I watched my mom and sister cry as they watched all the pecan trees around the property fall.

I feared the worst for my trailer and cried thinking about all the stuff I had lost. After living on the road for a year, I wasn't big on personal belongings but I really regretted not packing up the night before. We all underestimated the cane and it supercharged over the night. By then, the power was out and we couldn't properly be updated on what to do. It was life or death consequences.

After Hurricane Michael

After the storm passed, we walked toward our answer. We had to avoid downed live electric wires, broken glass, and sheet metal in every direction. We luckily got a visual that our trailer was still standing, although all the windows were broken and the exterior was completely destroyed. We still had a roof so I was happy. My animals were distraught and we didn't have power for 26 hot days but we survived. Our town is still rebuilding and sadly preparing for the next hurricane season.

Remnants of the amusement center are being hauled away but the legacy will live forever. One night I'd like to go explore the ruins but I know the area is heavily patrolled. My friend has an EVP machine and thermal camera and I'm sure we can get some answers to what hidden mysteries fall between the walls and down the lanes.

As for the voices in the woods, I may have a clue. Recently I interviewed a local military veteran who has done a lot of exploring in this region. He says that there are a few caves back off of the railroad and he has had some strange occurrences back there. He has seen weird flashes of lights, found unexplainable animal tracks and has also heard children's voices. He believes there is a chamber of secrets below the city.

I have no clue if the being was in the natural world or just some supernatural phenomenon. I have heard of Skinwalkers and Sasquatch calling people by name and in voices of loved ones but I feel the force in the woods was something not easily comprehensible by the human mind. I will never forget my time on the lanes, it was a dream come true.

CHAPTER 17
FINISHER

Me and the Great Sphinx

Madness will seep and creep onto our porch and will rip the door off the hinges. So make sure to have a back up plan for the deadbolt! Storms and surges of energy will trespass your land and try to take what's dear to our hearts. Mysteries and monsters are truly around the corner.

Please don't underestimate the value of safety. Remember to pack the necessary supplies and to check in with family members. A good friend might be the difference between life and death. A trip to the forest can be a joyous time but should always be taken seriously. There are animals and unexplained forces in the bush that require extra care.

People have vanished from locked cars, crowded bars, and one way streets. We need to stay diligent and look out for our brothers and sisters. We need to be aware of the strange anomalies that occur in these crises. The buddy system is important. These mysterious forces will do anything to divide the group. Remember to stick together.

Infrasound, dehydration, and telepathic abilities might be some of the reasons for confusion in the woods but forests are mazes of illusions by themselves. People have mysteriously fallen ill, been lured deep into treacherous regions, and totally lost their mind in the woods. Hikers have witnessed weird whispers and strange lights in the sky. Boulder fields, granite, portals, and quick sand have swallowed people up. Watch where you set up camp.

Phantom calls and ding dong ditchers stir up the night but burglaries ruin your sanity. I remember checking every window and door at least four times before bed. I slept with a knife under my pillow and with one eye open. There was no way to live. It had a lot to do with my journey moving south.

Living on the road showed me the value of a roof. Sleeping on the couch taught me the value of a door. When my car battery died, I was in need of a friendly face. I waited and waited while nobody came. I began to lose hope when a future friend pulled up. Dude pulled up and jumped my car. We chopped it up for a half hour about his paranormal encounters and they helped with my books.

The smallest city block in the world. Dothan, Alabama

Everything is a part of the chapter. I had to check

myself. I had to remind myself that it was all part of the story. It has all been written. Everything happens for a reason. Hardships are rewarded by balance. The sunniest days follow the rain. Pleasure wouldn't feel so good if it weren't for the pain.

I miss my house on Boston and living with my parents. I fought with my sister a lot but we also had many good times. We explored the woods and played a lot of whiffle ball with the neighbor Michael. My memories and pets will live on forever within those walls and grounds. I'm sure our energy is residual in Beebetown.

Sticky Fingers, the band that started the road trip.

I have doubled in depth and grown so much while moving out of state. I have been tested in ways that I could never have imagined. I am amazed by the twist and turns that the swamp state has taken me on.

Somehow I am pretty sure I manifested all of this long ago. Sam and I pictured ourselves moving out of state and look where we are now!

No matter where the road takes me, I know that my roots will remain. With my Irish blood, comes banshee sight. I know that strange vibrations will follow me and I will do my best to interpret them. I will spread awareness and hopefully that will provide a blanket of protection. Some monsters you cannot outrun, so come up with the next best plan.

Farewell my friends and I will see you on our next journey. Pack smart and check the weather. Keep a positive mindset and create a goal for the day. Focus and push toward your path. Your needs will be met in abundance if you are prepared to walk the walk. Remember every camp has a Crystal Lake, so bring a swimsuit... and a LIFEJACKET!

CHAPTER 18
LETTERS FROM FAMILY AND FRIENDS

Bonnie

I live in a semi haunted house, which has had its share of hauntings. My parents told me that when I was little, I would tell them to see "angels". Whether it was in church, school or on the street. I remember them vividly but I also remember when I stopped seeing "angels" and started to see darker figures. Around the time my papa (grandpa) died, in 4th grade. We were at his funeral and I remember all of the "angels" I was looking at , rising up into the church's ceiling, and I remember a dark feeling coming over me. I wasn't sure if it was because my grandfather passed, or because of what I was about to experience. I remember feeling frantic and wanting to tell someone but when it came to what I would see, I tried to keep it to myself , since it would literally scare the shit out of my parents, which at one point even got me blessed by a priest and my very religious grandma.

Sun and moon carvings in Warden's Ledges, Ohio

The end of 4th/5th grade I started becoming an angry atheist. I would curse at god for my odd child reasons, and would remember being very angry at "god". I became depressed, fearful of everything and had many more encounters with these dark figures. Most of these encounters would happen before I'd try to fall asleep. I would wake up with gashes in my stomach, that looked like a cat cutting me . I have mementoes of waking up on the opposite side of my room, from what felt like a panic attack. I started to believe that I slept and walked but that wasn't the case.

Princess Ledges, Ohio

I remember one night feeling like I was being choked in my bed , and trying to scream but couldn't. I felt my room feeling pitch black even though my bright Sponge Bob night light lit up the whole room. I remember the second I felt I could breathe again, running to my parents room, screaming, and crying hoping that they would once again watch over me as I tried to fall asleep. They were at that point fed up from how many times I've told them about these figures, and what I felt they were.

They told me to say Hail Mary over and over until I fall asleep . I remember pounding on their door screaming bloody murder and they thought it'd be best to not answer the door and let me cope with my own ghost/demons. I remember feeling how dark my room was and how I felt these figures around me as I prayed. I was shaking to the point I could have passed out from shock. In the corner of my old room, in crayon there is a writing of me praying to god saying I'd become a "believer" if he spared me and my family from these hauntings. I'm not sure exactly what it says exactly since the crayon is a bright color and I wrote it when I was laying down , so it's very messy, but it's still there to this day.

The Cross in the Bible in the wall

I remember staying up saying the Hail Mary till I finally knocked out. That was the last day I saw those figures, felt those figures, and heard those figures till around my freshman year of college . I have memories of how they used to call for me to come downstairs, or open the door. They had high pitch voices, almost sounding like children. I remember them always calling my name, and hiding myself under as many blankets as possible. I used to think, "If they couldn't see me, they wouldn't bother me". That was never the case, because they definitely continued to haunt me until the night my parents made me do the Hail Mary.

I have memories of my blanket trying to be pulled off me, and memories of my dad going downstairs to turn off the tv , that would turn on in the middle of the night flicker uncontrollably through different channels, which he'd say, "was my papa", because at my Nana's (grandmas) house , the same thing would happen. After the night of the Hail Marys, I eventually became a believer of god, but I unfortunately ended up becoming so afraid of it happening again that I eventually became paranoid of everything especially the night time.

I have many more stories/or details I didn't add but I tried to tie some all in briefly to the biggest night I've encountered. I sometimes like to picture ghosts as demons/angels Because from what I've encountered I've met some nice ones and some pretty shitty ones too. Hope that helps!

———

Pau

I was at the beach with my friends. We were just having a toke + some drinks. A friend of mine, let's call her Joy, got pretty drunk. She was all over the place, like emotionally - laughing-crying. And she's been my room-mate ever since so there's this little fact I know about her - she's AFRAID of the dark. Where we were at was just full of trees, and then the beach. Not many people, no lights, nothin. There are few kubos (huts) and the rest were just a few tents. Joy told us that she wanted to pee.

Pirate ship carving

The 'bathroom' was in the middle of the dark surrounded by tall trees. I'm like "No boo, that's too far and too dark! Just pee by the shore" besides, she was hella drunk and couldn't walk straight. She was adamant about peeing there, so I just went with her. Eventually she couldn't get to it so she just peed beside a kubo. I helped her with her bottoms and after all that hassle, she sits down and tells me that the trees are beautiful, and yes, I do agree that the trees are beautiful! Then she started crying again and pouring out her feelings. So I was just there with her. Friends by the beach went to us.

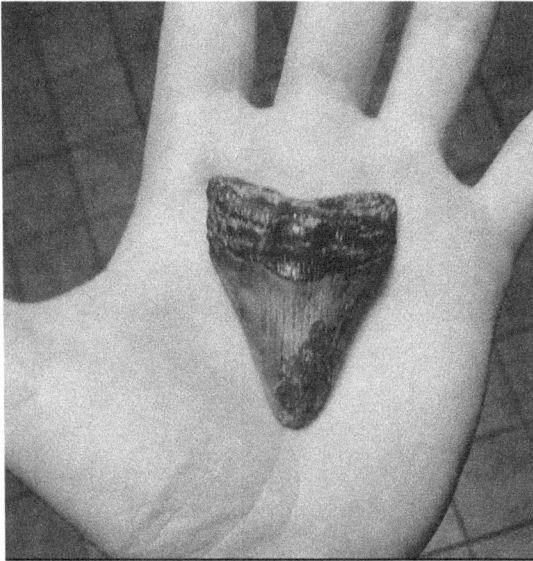

The Meg

She was still staring at the trees. And we were wondering what she was staring at. Looking around, kinda being cautious, yet amused. Then her eyes just stared into the abyss, eye level. She looked at one of us and said, "Sino ka" (Who are you) with a dead voice. That was the first time, man. I've seen her drunk in

MANY occasions but she never brought that vibe. Then she told us, "Wake up Matty". Then OKAY we woke him up. Didn't know why, but we did. It was odd cause they weren't that close.

As Matty wakes up he tells me, "This better be good, I'm getting my beauty rest" He looks over to Joy and is like "Oh gosh this can't be happening" It's like he knew what was happening. Okay that's when we all found out that he had a third eye or like this gift to see or feel other entities. Joy never knew that. Matty talks to Joy about it, and tells whatever entity that semi-possessed her to go away (in a friendly manner).

River Styx bridge in Ohio

We were around five to six people in a circle And started praying. Cause we were kinda scared. So eventually Joy was fine and just slept it off. So Matty explained to us that someone wanted to lure her into the woods.

We couldn't sleep that night, we were so scared that like when we woke up, she'd be gone. The next day, she woke up and we were like "YOOO do you remember ANYTHING from last night" Joy: why y'all lookin at me. So apparently there were stuff she couldn't remember, and her memory of that night was too blurry, and she said that it wasn't even from the alcohol.

———

Tyler

Basically my best friend in elementary school had a mom that was a witch and once, she messed up on whatever ceremony she was doing and I was at her house that night. I woke up to get water and when I was near her room I had this black aura that felt like it was taking over me. She woke up as soon as it happened and started chanting something then got me water and put me back to bed

———

Holley

My dog's food bowl was downstairs in the kitchen and my now ex was upstairs. He heard something and walked down and my dog's food bowl was upside down and was moving around the floor. Upstairs, when I'd sleep alone, all of my movies would fall onto the floor. If I didn't pick them up, they'd be in a different spot each morning. Some of my stuff would go missing and would be in an off the wall place. The doors slammed shut.

Aligator in Lousiana.

———

Johnny

When my great grandmother passed away ... we were all in the room with her when she died My father, my uncle, and my grandpa were all wearing watches - and there was a clock on the wall. A few minutes after she passed, we realized the clock in the wall had stopped at the time she died. And all their watches had stopped at nearly the same time. I just always looked at it as something that shows the energy that's inside us , and what it might mean to die.

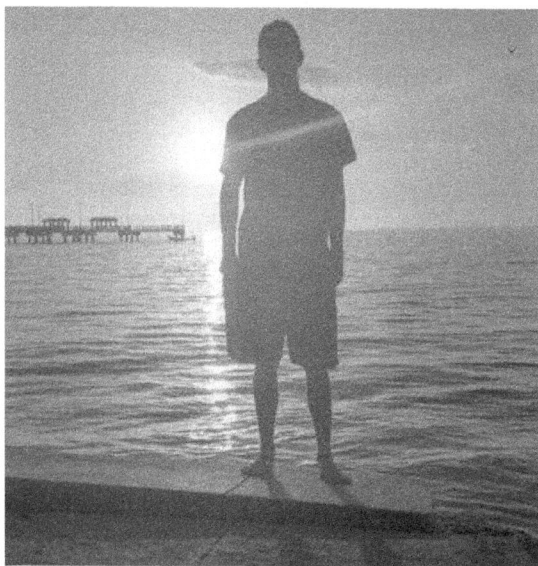

Desoto silhouette

In the months after passing, My mom was at home in

her room and the radio turned on all by itself. It was a song that she knew to be one of her grandmother's favorite songs. She turned the radio off and it turned right back on and she kept it on and let the rest of the song play.

Eastern Diamond Back Rattlesnake

Kathy

We stayed at the Conneaut Hotel. Which was supposedly haunted. Big fire there bride died there on her wedding night. What was left of the Ballroom still there in ruins when we were there.

Had a pretty creepy pic of Sarah in the room we

stayed in right on the lake shaped like an octagon. Kinda ghostlike. She looked like she was floating. I have to find it. I believe it had to do with something in developing the film. Long story.

Edward Scissorhands filming location, Lakeland, Florida

We almost had the hotel to ourselves. Walked through the whole thing. Went into just about any room we wanted, maintenance took us into a so-called haunted room. It was kinda creepy.

Castillo de San Marcos in St. Augustine, Florida

Babysitter

Famous masked wrestler of Florida

My dude Brandon has a haunted house. He grew up a couple houses down from your place in Boston. He's had doors slam and other weird shit. One of the previous owners hung himself in their garage.

———

Juan

Providence Canyon

My name is Juan and one night I was out feeding the animals and I just managed to look up and I seen this reddish orange line with a dot at the end in the dot wasn't flickering or anything but as it was moving up the line the line was disappearing as it was going behind it and then once it hit the end of the line it vanished and I freaked out because I've never seen anything like that before in my life

Sketch of The Grassman

———

Tony & Adriana

Driving on the road past the swamps, Tony came closer to a row of trees with a warning sign that a large crow was resting on. Thinking nothing much of the sight until they were halfway past the swamp, another warning sign appeared for the gas pumps buried beneath the soil with a similar crow perched on top of the sign. Tony thought it was weird to be able to see two crows nearby, but that was all. Finally reaching the edge of the swamp, a third crow was standing on a different warning sign, spread its wings and took flight towards the trees. It did a twisted turn with one wing wings clutched to it's stomach and the other spread out, it disappeared into the spaced out trees, leaving three feathers floating to the ground.

Haunted St. Lukes Church, Marianna, Florida.

For some weeks during the night Adriana would hear

a tune. The tune was loud and solemn, playing at a slow speed, it was creepy and somewhat comforting at the same time. During the day, she would try to find out the name of the tune on the Internet, but couldn't find anything. Every night for about a week, she would hear the tune as she was falling asleep. One day when she was spending time in her brother's room she unconsciously hummed the tune to herself when he asked what she was humming. She replied that she didn't know, it was just a tune that she would hear at night. Her brother then told her seriously that he recognized that tune. Asking what it was, he replied that it was a funeral tune that would be played during WW2. Not believing him, she denied what he said until he showed her a clip on youtube that played the same tune that she had been hearing. Shocked that she was hearing music for the dead at night, she went to bed fearfully that night, only to never hear the tune again.

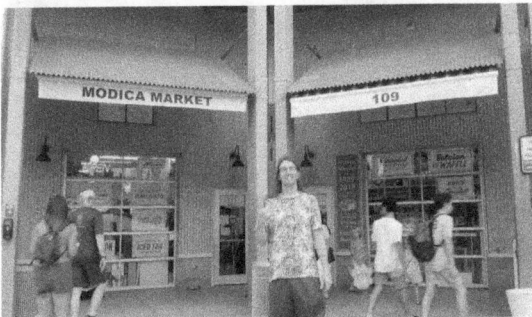

Monica Market from The Truman Show

Bryan

I had one of my best encounters last night. Was sitting around the fire by myself. Looked up and saw an eye shine about 7'5 feet tall. I pointed at it and waved to test it out. Then it went smoothly from 7'5 feet to 2 feet.

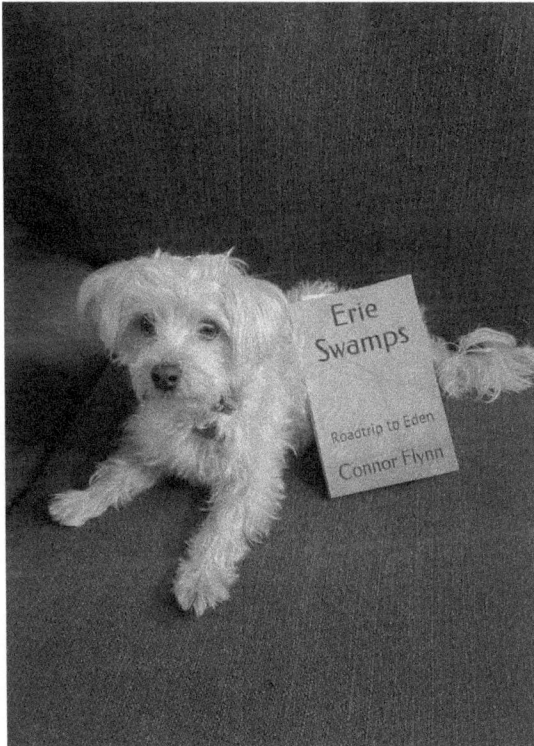

Our Angel up in heaven.

Weird symbols in a tree, Ocheesee, Florida

ABOUT THE AUTHOR

Connor Flynn is originally from the coast of Lake Erie and now resides in the Florida Panhandle. His love for outdoors and investigative journalism has led him down many paths of strange and unusual things. Flynn has appeared in films "Zillafoot" and "The Void Cat" and hosts a horror themed podcast. Catch Connor in the swamp or on the screen, he stays active in the field always waiting for a scream!

Visit him at his YouTube Channel below and on other social media platforms.

YouTube: https://www.youtube.com/channel/UCvcN_fkxz1wtjgwibEtF6qQ

ALSO BY CONNOR FLYNN

Erie Swamps: Road Trip to Eden

Big Brother, Bigfoot